THE NEW
MAYO CLINIC
COOKBOOK

CONCISE EDITION

THE NEW
MAYO CLINIC
COOKBOOK

CONCISE EDITION

Eating Well for Better Health

FOREWORD
Donald Hensrud, M.D., and Jennifer Nelson, R.D., Mayo Clinic

RECIPES
Cheryl Forberg, R.D., and Maureen Callahan, R.D.

PHOTOGRAPHS
Sheri Giblin

Mayo Clinic Health Information

CONTENTS

FOREWORD

It's a common belief that what tastes good and what's good for you are two different things. "At home we try to eat only healthy foods," a friend said recently at a party, as the appetizers were passed. "You know what that means—less flavor."

But as this new cookbook elegantly demonstrates, that doesn't need to be the case. What you eat does directly affect your health, as research has shown and our own clinical experience has confirmed. At the same time, we've come to believe that eating well and eating healthfully can and should go hand in hand. Food that is deliciously rich in flavor doesn't have to be bad for you. Moreover, cooking with nutritious ingredients—such as vegetables, fruits, and whole grains—may actually lower your risk of developing many diseases, from heart disease to cancer. That's an important concept behind this remarkable new collection.

These recipes make up the first cookbook based on the Mayo Clinic Healthy Weight Pyramid. Although the pyramid was designed as a weight-control tool, it can easily be put to use by everyone interested in eating wisely for better health. This cookbook adheres to the pyramid's principles while showcasing the foods that provide an array of valuable nutrients. It also offers an abundance of great-tasting dishes that are low in "energy density"—that is, they're filling and satisfying but low in calories—so you can eat well without feeling either guilty or deprived. We know you'll enjoy cooking from this collection of versatile recipes, and we are excited to be able to offer them to you.

Donald Hensrud, M.D., and Jennifer Nelson, R.D., Mayo Clinic

Greek Salad, page 61

ELEGANTLY SIMPLE IDEAS FOR HEALTHY EATING

Today we understand that good food is crucial to good health. People who regularly enjoy meals made with a variety of healthful ingredients may lower their chances of developing heart disease, diabetes, many kinds of cancer, osteoporosis, obesity, age-related vision loss, digestive disorders, and more.

But deciding to eat wisely doesn't mean having to seek out unusual "health foods" such as broccoli sprouts and wheatgrass. It doesn't mean denying yourself desserts and other delicacies you love. And it doesn't have to be complicated or expensive. After all, some of the world's most tempting dishes are built around the season's best produce, prepared simply to bring out the fullest flavors.

You'll find plenty of recipes here to match your tastes. Simple or fancy, familiar or adventurous, the 50 dishes in this book are designed to be as satisfying as they are good for you. In the following pages, you'll discover a whole new philosophy of cooking and eating, along with helpful suggestions on menu planning and practical insights on the ingredients themselves. To eat well, just help yourself.

Flavor comes first. The new approach to eating well is full of enjoyment and satisfaction.

Summer Vegetable Soup, page 70

A NEW PHILOSOPHY OF COOKING

We enjoy an abundance of food choices unparalleled in history—just take a look around in the aisles of a well-stocked supermarket. With so many great ingredients near at hand, it's easy to prepare dishes that not only are a pleasure to serve and eat but also benefit your health. The new kitchen philosophy, reflected in the recipes in this book, is to say yes to the extraordinary variety of foods that taste terrific and are terrific for you.

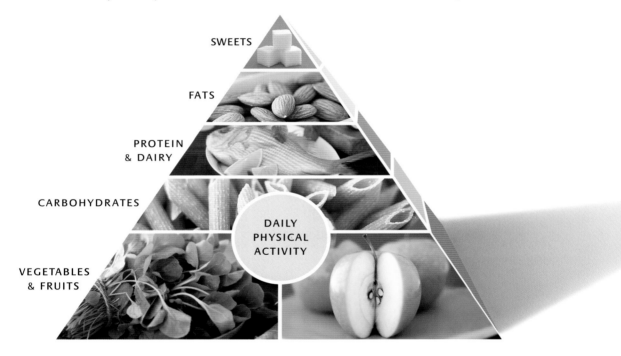

The Mayo Clinic Healthy Weight Pyramid

The Mayo Clinic Healthy Weight Pyramid depicts the nutritional principles of a regular pattern of healthy eating. The pyramid's sections represent six food groups. The bigger the block, the more servings from that group you'll want in your meals.

To build everyday menus, start at the pyramid's base with ample veg-etables and fruits. Include plenty of high-fiber carbohydrates, then add smaller portions of protein, dairy, and fats. Go easy on sweets, and engage in daily physical activity.

Note that unlike some of the other healthy-eating pyramids you may have seen, this one rests on a broad foundation of vegetables and fruits, rather than grains and other carbohydrates, in recognition of the many scientific findings about their health benefits.

If you regularly enjoy a variety of colorful produce, from broccoli to berries, you have already taken an important step toward choosing a full mix of health-promoting foods.

How the Pyramid Can Help

People who adopt the pyramid's principles may lower their risk of several illnesses, including heart disease, diabetes, and cancer. How?

Vegetables and fruits are endowed with fiber, vitamins, and antioxidants, which many experts believe work together to help fight disease. Fruits, in addition, can satisfy urges for sweets that are full of fat and sugar. Carbohydrates—and especially whole grains—are likewise rich in disease-fighting nutrients, and there are many healthful protein sources.

Even the right kinds of fats can help fend off illness, although they're high in calories—the reason they're given less space in the pyramid.

Healthy Eating Basics

- Think variety and balance
- Favor vegetables and fruits
- Eat more whole grains
- Choose smart proteins
- Use good types of fat
- Save sweets for treats

Why It's Called the Healthy Weight Pyramid

Without an eye to how much we eat, it's easy to take in too many calories, the food energy that fuels our bodies. Excess calories turn to excess weight, a health concern of its own.

To maintain a healthy weight, try to eat only as much food as your body can burn in a day—1,600 to 2,800 calories' worth for most adults.

The goals in the chart at right and on the following pages are based on a daily average of 2,000 calories.

Within that calorie goal, it's easy to build meals using the pyramid's food groups. Aim for the targets at right—but don't worry if you don't always hit them. The ultimate goal is a long-term pattern of healthy eating.

Daily Servings Goals

VEGETABLES	5 or more per day
FRUITS	5 or more per day
CARBOHYDRATES	8 per day
PROTEIN & DAIRY	7 per day
FATS	5 per day

ABOVE **Baby Beets and Carrots with Dill,** page 28; **Seared Salmon with Cilantro-Cucumber Salsa,** page 112

HOW TO USE THIS BOOK

To help you cook, serve, and eat a well-balanced variety of healthy foods, each of the 50 recipes in this book is accompanied by two types of charts. The first includes a breakdown showing exactly how far one portion of a dish moves you toward reaching the Daily Servings Goals that accompany the Mayo Clinic Healthy Weight Pyramid. The second chart is a standard nutritional analysis that includes calories (kilojoules) and several other important nutrients (see the page at right). Remember, it's not a single dish or menu but your overall eating pattern that matters most to your health.

THE SERVINGS DIAGRAM

Near the top of every recipe page in this cookbook, you will see Pyramid Servings, a graphic with several rows of shaded and unshaded circles that visually represent how the dish stacks up against the Daily Servings Goals listed in the chart at the bottom of page 11.

○ Unshaded circles show the total daily servings recommended.

● Shaded circles show how many servings that recipe provides.

◀ Left arrows with Vegetables and Fruits mean there's no daily limit.

Pyramid Servings		
VEGETABLES	◀ ○○○○●
FRUITS	◀ ○○○○●
CARBOHYDRATES	○○○○○○○○○
PROTEIN & DAIRY	○○○○○○○
FATS	○○○○●

 SWEETS SMALL IS BEAUTIFUL

You won't find daily servings goals for sweets, even though they're at the pyramid's peak. That's because candies, cakes, and other goodies made with refined sugar or honey and usually lots of fat are high-calorie foods that are low in nutrients—what experts call empty calories. That's not to say they're off-limits. To satisfy your sweet tooth in moderation—up to an average of 125 calories a day—simply enjoy fresh fruit sometimes instead of prepared sweets or desserts. Here are some helpful calorie counts.

1 teaspoon sugar
16 calories (67 kilojoules)

1 homemade oatmeal-raisin cookie
65 calories (272 kilojoules)

4 ounces (125 g) sorbet
95 calories (398 kilojoules)

1 ounce (28 g) semisweet chocolate
135 calories (566 kilojoules)

THE NUTRITIONAL ANALYSIS

The recipes in this book incorporate a range of healthful ingredients and also meet widely accepted standards for heart-healthy menus. To present complete nutrition data, each recipe has been analyzed by a registered dietitian, enabling you to compare these dishes to those in other cookbooks and to packaged foods in the market. Nutrient measurements are in grams (g) and milligrams (mg). All measures have been rounded to the nearest whole number.

PER SERVING	
calories	105
kilojoules	439
protein	3 g
carbohydrate	14 g
total fat	5 g
saturated fat	1 g
monounsaturated fat	3 g
cholesterol	2 mg
sodium	170 mg
fiber	4 g

- Any ingredient labeled "optional" is counted in the nutritional analysis.

- Wine and other alcoholic beverages included as ingredients are optional.

- Where two or more ingredient choices are given, only the first is counted.

- Measurements reported as < 1 (less than one) fall between 0 and 1.

BELOW Photos, such as this salad of mixed greens, show one portion. The Pyramid Servings chart depicts how many standard servings each portion provides. The Per Serving box below it has full nutrition facts.

Mesclun Salad with Radishes, Avocado, and Blood Oranges

The mix of gourmet salad greens called mesclun may include oakleaf lettuce, arugula (rocket), frisée, mizuna, mâche, radicchio, and sorrel. Here, it is brightened with the red flesh of blood oranges.

SERVES 6

2 small blood oranges or other oranges

1 tablespoon rice vinegar

½ teaspoon Dijon mustard

1 tablespoon extra-virgin olive oil

¼ teaspoon salt

¼ teaspoon freshly ground pepper

6 cups (6 oz/185 g) mesclun or mixed young salad greens

4 red radishes, trimmed and very thinly sliced

½ small avocado, peeled and thinly sliced

2 tablespoons crumbled blue cheese

Working with 1 orange at a time, cut a thin slice off the top and the bottom, exposing the flesh. Stand the orange upright and, using a sharp knive, thickly cut off the peel, following the contour of the fruit and removing all the white pith and membrane. Holding the orange over a small bowl, carefully cut along both sides of each section to free it from the membrane. As you work, discard any seeds and let the sections and any juice fall into the bowl. Repeat with the second orange. When both oranges are sectioned, squeeze the membranes into the bowl to extract all of the juice.

To make the vinaigrette, in a small bowl, whisk together 2 tablespoons of the captured blood orange juice, the vinegar, and the mustard. While whisking, slowly add the olive oil in a thin stream until emulsified. Whisk in the salt and pepper. Reserve any remaining orange juice for another use.

In a large bowl, combine the mesclun, radishes, and orange sections. Pour the vinaigrette over the salad and toss gently to mix well and coat evenly.

To serve, divide the salad among individual plates. Top each portion with slices of avocado and sprinkle with the cheese.

Pyramid Servings

VEGETABLES	4 ○○○○●
FRUITS	4 ○○○○●
CARBOHYDRATES	0 ○○○○○○
PROTEIN & DAIRY	0 ○○○○○○
FATS	0 ○○○●

PER SERVING	
calories	105
kilojoules	439
protein	3 g
total fat	5 g
saturated fat	1 g
monounsaturated fat	3 g
cholesterol	2 mg
sodium	170mg
fiber	4 g

Salads 65

VEGETABLES & FRUITS

To enjoy a full mix of health-promoting foods, pick a variety of colors from the produce bin.

It's hardly news that vegetables and fruits are good for you. The real news is why. More and more is being learned about how fresh produce, beyond its rich stores of vitamins, can supply us with substances that help ward off illnesses.

Strong evidence is stacking up that people who regularly eat generous helpings of vegetables—a *variety* of vegetables—run a lower risk of developing heart disease, a leading killer of American adults.

Most vegetables are loaded with the antioxidants beta-carotene and vitamin C. Antioxidants can be important because these substances play a role in inhibiting molecules called oxygen free radicals, which can damage healthy cells in the body. Vegetables are also key sources of essential minerals, including potassium and magnesium. Many are rich in health-enhancing fiber, and some even have calcium. In addition, researchers have identified another class of substances in these plants—called phytochemicals—that appear to offer some protection against cancer.

Tomatoes, for instance, get their red color from lycopene. Studies suggest that getting plenty of this phytochemical may lower prostate cancer risk.

Fruits, like many vegetables, have an abundance of fiber—not to mention a long list of healthful antioxidants, including vitamin C.

Researchers have also discovered that many fruits contain generous amounts of flavonoids, substances that apparently work together to lower the risk of cancer and heart disease. Some fruits and vegetables contain the antioxidants lutein and zeaxanthin, which may help guard against certain conditions related to aging, such as the eye disease macular degeneration. Oranges are rich in a little-known compound called beta-sitosterol, which is believed to help lower blood cholesterol.

These many benefits are the reason why under the pyramid there's no limit on the daily servings of fresh and frozen vegetables and fruits. The exceptions are dried fruits and fruit juices, which measure for measure are much higher in calories than the fresh fruits from which they're made.

ABOVE LEFT Red grapes are an abundant source of a phytochemical called resveratrol, thought to help shield against cardiovascular disease and cancer.

ABOVE RIGHT Cruciferous vegetables such as broccoli and cabbage are rich in compounds that are believed to help fend off certain forms of cancer.

THE GOAL

5 OR MORE VEGETABLE AND 5 OR MORE FRUIT SERVINGS A DAY

A vegetable serving is about 25 calories; a fruit serving, 60 calories.

GETTING THERE

A DAY'S MENU MIGHT INCLUDE (EACH ITEM IS 1 SERVING)

1 tomato or 8 cherry tomatoes	1 orange, apple, or banana
2 cups (2 oz/60 g) salad greens	½ grapefruit
½ cup (2 oz/60 g) carrot sticks	½ cup (3 oz/90 g) grapes
1 cup (2 oz/60 g) broccoli	1 cup (4 oz/125 g) berries

IN THE KITCHEN

A FEW RECIPES TO TRY

62   Yellow Pear and Cherry Tomato Salad

75   Fresh Tomato Soup with Crispy Herb Toasts

41   Steamed Summer Squash with Warm Leek Vinaigrette

57   Ambrosia with Coconut and Toasted Almonds

49   Mixed Fresh Berries with Ginger Sauce

LEFT A half-cup (2 oz/60 g) of Mixed Fresh Berries with Ginger Sauce (page 49), made with fresh blackberries, raspberries, and red currants, equals 1 serving.

 DAILY ACTIVITY BE A MOVER AND A SHAKER

Staying active is just as important as nutritious food for a healthy life. Physical activity burns calories, making it easier to maintain your weight. It's also just plain good for you, strengthening your heart and lungs. Inactivity, on the other hand, is clearly dangerous—perhaps as bad for you as smoking. As little as 30 minutes to an hour of brisk walking most days of the week can help reduce your risk of heart disease and stroke as well as several forms of cancer.

- Take a brisk walk around the neighborhood in the morning or in the evening after work.

- Find activities you enjoy, such as hiking, swimming, tennis, throwing a Frisbee, playing catch with the kids, or hitting the trail with the dog.

- Do errands on foot when you don't have to drive.

CARBOHYDRATES ▲

The message is nearly this simple: the less refined a high-carbohydrate food, the better it is for you.

Think of every kind of food containing carbohydrates laid out in a line. At one end are whole wheat, oats, and brown rice. In the middle sit white flour, white rice, potatoes, and pastas. And at the far end are cookies, candies, and soft drinks.

The diverse foods in that spectrum incorporate all three kinds of carbohydrates: fiber, starch, and sugar. It's not hard to point to the healthy and less healthy ends—unrefined whole grains on one hand, refined sugar on the other.

But the health pros and cons of many items in the middle aren't so clear. Rice, pasta, bread, and potatoes can all shift depending on how they're produced and served.

Consider, for example, white and whole-wheat (wholemeal) breads. Both begin as whole grains, as do both white and brown rice. That whole, or unrefined, grain consists of outer layers, known as the bran and germ, surrounding a starchy interior, called the endosperm.

Whole grains abound with nutrients. Some are rich in vitamin E, an antioxidant that has many health benefits. Others contain estrogenlike substances that may help protect against some forms of cancer.

During processing, however, the bran and germ are refined away, and by the time the wheat has become a loaf of white bread or the rice is a steaming white side dish, they've lost many of their vitamins and almost all of their fiber. That's why it's wise to choose whole-grain breads, pastas, and cereals, and to serve brown rice instead of white.

Similarly, the edible skins so often removed from potatoes and sweet potatoes are full of nutrients and fiber. (For more information, see Fiber: The Two Types and Their Benefits, opposite.)

Of course, many foods not always thought of as carbohydrates contain significant amounts of fiber, starch, and sugar—not only vegetables and fruits but also sweets, chips, and other processed products. The key word is *whole*. Generally, the message is that simple: The less refined a carbohydrate food, the better it is for you.

ABOVE LEFT Bulgur, a type of cracked wheat, is a quick-cooking grain with a mild, nutty flavor and a respectable amount of fiber. It's good in side dishes and salads.

ABOVE RIGHT Whole-wheat (wholemeal) pastas are made from wheat grains with their germ intact. They contain more vitamins and fiber than standard pastas.

THE GOAL

8 CARBOHYDRATE SERVINGS A DAY, MOSTLY WHOLE GRAINS

A carbohydrate serving is about 70 calories.

GETTING THERE

A DAY'S MENU MIGHT INCLUDE (EACH ITEM IS 1 SERVING)

½ cup (1½ oz/45 g) dry cereal 2 cups (½ oz/15 g) fat-free popcorn

½ whole-grain English muffin ½ cup (3 oz/90 g) cooked pasta

1 slice whole-grain bread ½ medium baked sweet potato

½ cup (3 oz/90 g) cooked bulgur 1 oatmeal cookie

IN THE KITCHEN

A FEW RECIPES TO TRY

88 Three-Grain Raspberry Muffins

85 Savory Buckwheat Pilaf with Toasted Spices

79 Spinach Lasagne with Sun-Dried Tomato Sauce

81 Orzo with Cherry Tomatoes, Capers, and Lemon

82 Double-Corn Spoon Bread

LEFT **Made with wheat bran, oats, and cornmeal, each Three-Grain Raspberry Muffin equals 1 carbohydrate serving, plus 1 fruit serving from the fresh berries.**

FIBER THE TWO TYPES AND THEIR BENEFITS

Grains, fruits, and vegetables all contain a kind of carbohydrate, called fiber, that resists digestive enzymes and cannot be absorbed by your body. There are two main types—insoluble and soluble—both of which are found in varying amounts in most plants. Fiber-rich foods slow the uptake of glucose, thus helping to keep blood sugar steady. Research suggests that the more fiber people get from grains, the lower their risk of type 2 diabetes. Experts recommend consuming 20 to 35 grams of fiber a day.

- Insoluble fiber—called roughage—is coarse, indigestible plant material best known for promoting healthy digestion. Many common vegetables and whole grains contain significant amounts.

- Soluble fiber—vegetable matter that turns goopy in water—helps lower blood cholesterol levels. Barley, oats, and beans contain notable amounts.

PROTEIN & DAIRY

Many beans and legumes have so much protein that when they're on the menu, meat can step aside.

Protein is essential to human life. Your skin, bone, muscle, and organ tissues are made up of protein, and it's present in your blood, too. Protein is also found in foods, many of animal origin.

But despite what you may have heard, it's not necessary or even desirable to eat meat every day.

Although rich in protein, many cuts of chicken, turkey, beef, lamb, and pork are too high in saturated fat and cholesterol to include regularly for good health (see Healthful and Harmful Fats, page 21). Remember, other everyday ingredients, including low-fat dairy products, fish and shellfish, and many plant foods, furnish protein, too.

Legumes—namely beans, lentils, and peas—are also an excellent source. And because they have no cholesterol and very little fat, they're great for filling out or replacing dishes made with poultry or meat.

Unlike meat, beans actually help lower the "bad" form of cholesterol, and the minerals they contain help control blood pressure.

You may also have heard that beans' protein is "incomplete," meaning it lacks essential amino acids that meats provide. That's true; among legumes, only soybeans have protein containing all the amino acids. However, the missing nutrients are plentiful in other plant foods, so people who lighten up on meat can easily get all they need.

Likewise, nonfat and low-fat dairy products, especially milk and yogurt, can help supply you with protein. On top of that, milk is rich in calcium and is fortified with vitamin D, which helps bodies absorb that important bone-building mineral.

And don't neglect fish and shellfish. Not only are they fine protein sources, but some supply omega-3 fatty acids. Research suggests that most people would benefit by eating at least two servings of fish a week.

The omega-3 fats in fish help lower triglycerides, fat particles in the blood that appear to raise heart disease risk, and may also help prevent dangerous heartbeat disturbances known as arrhythmias, improve immune function, and help regulate blood pressure.

ABOVE LEFT Yogurt, like milk and other dairy products, delivers protein and calcium, a bone-building mineral that may also help protect against high blood pressure, stroke, and kidney stones.

ABOVE RIGHT Lentils—including the French green variety here—are legumes, plants whose seeds develop in pods. Legumes are a source of folate, or folic acid, a B-vitamin that helps prevent some birth defects.

THE GOAL

7 LOW-FAT PROTEIN AND DAIRY SERVINGS A DAY

A protein serving is about 110 calories.

GETTING THERE

A DAY'S MENU MIGHT INCLUDE (EACH ITEM IS 1 SERVING)

1 cup (8 fl oz/250 ml) low-fat milk	2 ounces (60 g) lean beef
1 cup (8 oz/250 g) nonfat yogurt	3 ounces (90 g) fish or shellfish
¼ cup (1¼ oz/40 g) feta cheese	½ cup (3 oz/90 g) cooked beans
½ cup (4 oz/125 g) tofu	1½–2 oz (45–60 g) skinless chicken

IN THE KITCHEN

A FEW RECIPES TO TRY

105 Classic Boston Baked Beans

122 Chicken Stir-Fry with Eggplant and Basil

103 Sesame-Crusted Tofu

110 Pan-Braised Swordfish with Feta

123 Beef Stew with Fennel and Shallots

LEFT **Each helping of Sesame-Crusted Tofu provides 2 protein and dairy servings and contains enough green (spring) onions to provide 1 vegetable serving.**

SODIUM A LIGHT HAND WITH SALT

Sodium occurs in many foods, from milk and cheeses to crackers and pie. It also makes up about 40 percent of table salt. For some people, consuming too much sodium raises blood pressure, and elevated blood pressure increases the risk of heart disease and stroke.

Nutrition experts suggest aiming for no more than 2,400 milligrams of sodium a day—about what's in a teaspoon of salt—from processed foods and from what you add at the stove and table.

- Keep an eye out for the hidden sodium in breakfast cereals, dairy products, chips, and breads.

- Instead of heavily salted canned and processed foods, choose fresh or frozen fish, poultry, or meat, and make your own soups.

- Go easy with the salt shaker. Your tastes buds will adjust.

FATS

Avocados, olives, nuts, seeds, and vegetable oils, used wisely, can actually help prevent heart disease.

The idea that all fat is bad is so widespread that many people are surprised to hear health experts say some kinds can be beneficial. Studies over the past two decades have confirmed that people who replace much of the animal fat in their meals with liquid vegetable oils stand a good chance of bringing down their blood cholesterol levels, thereby lowering their risk of cardiovascular disease.

Other findings suggest that the people who favor foods made with liquid oils, such as canola and olive oils, over ones with solid shortenings and margarines may derive similar health benefits.

Meats, seafoods, and many dairy products can be fatty, of course, which is to say that some foods traditionally considered proteins can add significant fat to a day's meals.

Fats from all sources—including those in the pyramid's sweets and protein and dairy sections—are best held to 9 to 13 servings a day, with 5 of those from foods in the pyramid's fats section.

Keep in mind, however, that the pyramid's fats section addresses only the high-fat ingredients often *added* to a day's meals. These include salad dressings, cooking oils, butter, and high-fat plant foods, such as avocado, olives, seeds, and nuts.

Most of these foods are good for you. Nuts, for instance, contain a type of oil that helps keep hearts and arteries free of harmful deposits. They also deliver other nutrients, including protein, thiamin, niacin, folate, selenium, and vitamin E.

But while nuts and vegetable oils may be beneficial, they're best used in moderation. A tablespoon of peanut butter weighs in at nearly 100 calories; a tablespoon of olive oil, 140. In other words, the goal is to use *just enough* of these naturally high-fat ingredients.

On the other hand, some fats are best kept to a minimum. Saturated fat, largely from foods of animal origin, has long been known to raise LDL ("bad") cholesterol and lower HDL ("good") cholesterol. But now research has shown that foods high in trans fats, common in processed foods, have a similar impact on cholesterol levels (see Healthful and Harmful Fats, opposite).

ABOVE LEFT Almonds, like other nuts, have abundant protein, making them a fine companion for vegetables in stir-fries, casseroles, and other dishes.

ABOVE RIGHT Avocados are a rich source of beta-sitosterol, a compound that may help lower blood cholesterol.

THE GOAL

5 ADDED FAT SERVINGS A DAY, MOSTLY MONOUNSATURATED

A fat serving is about 45 calories.

GETTING THERE

A DAY'S MENU MIGHT INCLUDE (EACH ITEM IS 1 SERVING)

7 almonds	9 large olives
4 walnut or pecan halves	3 slices avocado
1½ teaspoons peanut butter	2 teaspoons mayonnaise
1 tablespoon sunflower seeds	1 teaspoon canola or olive oil

IN THE KITCHEN

A FEW RECIPES TO TRY

33 Warm Potato Salad

34 Asparagus with Hazelnut Gremolata

65 Mesclun Salad with Radishes, Avocado, and Blood Oranges

131 Almond and Apricot Biscotti

132 Date-Walnut Cake with Warm Honey Sauce

LEFT **Chopped walnuts give each slice of Date-Walnut Cake with Warm Honey Sauce its 1 serving of added fat. Fresh Medjool dates contribute 2 servings of fruit.**

HEALTHFUL AND HARMFUL FATS EASY DOES IT

Eating wisely used to mean cutting back on all fat, but health experts now believe that some varieties of fat, used lightly, can actually be beneficial.

- Monounsaturates, in nuts, avocados, canola oil, and olive oil, help lower blood levels of LDL cholesterol, a cause of heart attacks and strokes. They also help keep arteries clear by maintaining levels of helpful HDL cholesterol.

- Polyunsaturates, including corn and soy oils, also keep harmful LDL cholesterol levels down. Among them are the heart-healthy omega-3 fats in fish, flaxseed, soybeans, tofu, walnuts, and walnut oil.

- Saturated fats, from meats, dairy products, and tropical oils, raise blood levels of LDL cholesterol. Limit these by using low-fat dairy products and by combining lean meats with vegetables and grains.

- Trans fats, found in hydrogenated vegetable oils in cookies, crackers, and deep-fried foods, may be even more harmful than saturated fats.

ARE YOU EATING WELL?

To see how your current food choices match up with the new philosophy of cooking and eating, answer the ten questions below and note your responses. Instead of an exact rating or score, you'll receive a broad view of the way you cook and eat—a view that can guide you toward making some basic choices for better health.

1 How many servings of vegetables do you eat in a typical day? (A serving is 2 cups [2 oz/60 g] of leafy greens, 1 cup [2 oz/60 g] of broccoli florets.)
- **A** four or more
- **B** two or three
- **C** one or none

2 How many servings of fruit do you eat in a typical day? (A serving is usually one small piece.)
- **A** three or more
- **B** two
- **C** one

3 How often does fish appear on your weekly menu?
- **A** two or more times
- **B** once
- **C** rarely or never

4 When you shop for bread, pasta, and rice, how often do you buy the whole-grain versions?
- **A** always
- **B** sometimes
- **C** rarely or never

5 Which of the following are you most likely to use?
- **A** canola or olive oil
- **B** corn oil
- **C** butter or margarine

6 How often during a typical week do you eat out and order hamburgers, cheese-rich pizzas, or sandwiches layered with meat and cheese?
- **A** not more than once
- **B** two or three times
- **C** four or more times

7 A dinner of 2 cups (12 oz/375 g) of cooked pasta in a tomato sauce is how many servings?
- **A** four
- **B** not sure
- **C** one

8 What kind of milk do you usually drink?
- **A** fat-free milk or soy milk
- **B** 1 or 2 percent
- **C** whole milk or none

9 What are you most likely to reach for when you're thirsty?
- **A** water
- **B** fruit juice
- **C** regular sweetened soda

10 What's your usual snack?
- **A** nuts, fruit, or carrot or celery sticks
- **B** energy bars or other "healthy" sweets
- **C** potato chips, pretzels, or cookies

A **IF YOU COUNT MOSTLY A'S** among your answers, congratulations. You're well on your way to healthy eating.

B **IF YOU COUNT MOSTLY B'S AND C'S,** your menu could use a tune-up. You'll find plenty of tips and great-tasting recipes in the following pages.

C **IF YOU ANSWERED WITH MOSTLY C'S AND FEW A'S,** it's time for some fresh ideas about good food. See Ten Easy Steps to Healthier Eating, opposite.

TEN EASY STEPS TO HEALTHIER EATING

A few simple changes can make a big difference in the nutrition profile of your daily meals.

1 Have at least one serving of fruit at each meal and more as snacks during the day.

2 Switch from low-fiber breakfast cereal to lower-sugar, higher-fiber alternatives.

3 Lighten your milk by moving down one step in fat content—from whole to 2 percent, for instance, or from 1 percent to fat-free.

4 Cook with olive, canola, or other vegetable oil instead of butter or margarine whenever you can.

5 Choose coarse whole-grain breads, switch to brown rice, and experiment with whole-wheat (wholemeal) flour when baking.

6 Include at least two servings of vegetables at lunch.

7 Have at least two vegetable servings at dinner.

8 Have fish as a main course at least twice a week.

9 Serve fresh fruit for dessert.

10 Replace high-calorie sweetened beverages with water, iced tea, or unsweetened fruit juices.

ABOVE LEFT **HAVE FISH AS A MAIN COURSE AT LEAST TWICE A WEEK.** Seafood dishes such as Mahimahi with Macadamia Nut Crust, page 109, not only provide protein but also furnish omega-3 fatty acids, oils that appear to help prevent heart ailments.

LEFT **SERVE FRESH FRUIT FOR DESSERT.** Colorful desserts such as Summer Fruit Gratin, page 126, make it a pleasure to add servings of fruit to your daily menu. Fruits are rich with compounds that help fend off cancer and heart disease.

HOW TO PLAN A MENU

This book is designed to make it easy to put balanced meals on the table. Not only does every dish meet sound nutrition guidelines, but the recipes are also arranged to correspond generally to the Mayo Clinic Healthy Weight Pyramid. You'll find three dinner menus on the facing page, each showing its servings of vegetables and fruits, carbohydrates, protein and dairy, and fats. Use the following principles to plan your own weeknight dinners and weekend celebrations.

REMEMBER THE PYRAMID

As a way to approach nutrition goals, try to include more than one serving from most food groups in most menus. In thinking about fruits, for instance, aim for at least one serving at breakfast, lunch, and dinner, plus two more as snacks during the day. To get plenty of vegetables every day, build lunches and dinners that incorporate two or three servings each. Getting there is actually easier than it sounds, because many dishes contain more than one vegetable serving (for examples, see page 15).

ABOVE **Protein-rich Roasted Rack of Lamb with Parsley Crust, page 120, is balanced with Asparagus with Hazelnut Gremolata, page 34, and roasted potatoes.**

PLAN BY THE WEEK

Don't get hung up on hitting exact daily servings goals. If on Monday you don't reach your fruits target, add an extra serving or two on Tuesday. Boost your weekly greens and whole grains totals by making some lunches and dinners vegetarian—a strategy that will also help you move toward healthful proteins, such as beans and lentils, tofu, and low-fat dairy products.

MAKE PLEASURE A PRIORITY

While it's gratifying to know you're reaching nutrition targets, number crunching can become a chore. Good food is one of life's great pleasures, which is to say that eating well is not about deprivation. It's about enjoying superb ingredients with remarkable health benefits. So when cooking, take advantage of their flavors, colors, and textures to present pleasing dishes.

CHANGE WITH THE SEASONS

Although it's possible to purchase tomatoes in January and summer squash in March, they may not be truly fresh. Whenever you can, look for recently harvested produce—asparagus, peas, and cherries in spring; peaches, sweet corn, and tomatoes in midsummer; apples, pears, and beets in fall—and you'll enjoy the freshest and most nutritious foods available. Even in winter months you can shop for freshness by seeking out winter squash, red cabbage, and root vegetables such as carrots, turnips, and sweet potatoes.

BE ADVENTUROUS

Discovering new foods and flavors is part of the joy of cooking, so don't be afraid to explore unfamiliar foods and cooking techniques. Some of the world's most intriguing ingredients—buckwheat, edamame, sun-dried tomatoes, tofu—are as healthful as they are delicious. Bear in mind that the best way to get the full range of health benefits is to plan menus with a wide variety of nutritious foods.

SUMMER FARE

Yellow Pear and Cherry
Tomato Salad
62

Warm Potato Salad
33

Black Bean Burgers
with Chipotle Ketchup
95

Mixed Berries with
Ginger Sauce
49

ABOVE A hearty black bean burger
anchors a grain- and legume-rich
dinner with a warm-weather feeling.

Pyramid Servings per Menu

VEGETABLES	◀○○○○●
FRUITS	◀○○○○●
CARBOHYDRATES	○○○○○●●●
PROTEIN & DAIRY	○○○○○●●
FATS	○○●●●

WINTRY WEEKEND SUPPER

Beef Stew with
Fennel and Shallots
123

Baby Beets and
Carrots with Dill
28

Two-Potato Gratin
43

Baked Apples with Cherries
and Almonds
54

ABOVE Baked apples, a classic dish
of the fall harvest season, round out
this satifying all-American dinner.

Pyramid Servings per Menu

VEGETABLES	◀○●●●●
FRUITS	◀○○○●●
CARBOHYDRATES	○○○○○●●●
PROTEIN & DAIRY	○○○○○○●
FATS	○○●●●

ENTERTAINING EVENING

Fresh Tomato Soup
with Crispy Herb Toasts
75

Roasted Rack of Lamb
with Parsley Crust
120

Asparagus with
Hazelnut Gremolata
34

Orange Slices
with Citrus Syrup
50

ABOVE Fresh asparagus, which
appears in markets in spring, sets
the mood for a celebratory dinner.

Pyramid Servings per Menu

VEGETABLES	◀○○○●●
FRUITS	◀○○●●●
CARBOHYDRATES	○○○○○○●
PROTEIN & DAIRY	○○○○●●●
FATS	○○○○○

Vegetables

In their pleasing variety of flavors, colors, and textures, vegetables are the foundation of healthy eating.

Baby Beets and Carrots with Dill

SERVES 6

Red and yellow baby beets, particularly those varieties with striped flesh, make this dish special. If you can't find them, full-grown beets and carrots will also work. Simply cut them into small pieces.

Pyramid Servings

VEGETABLES	◀○○○○●
FRUITS	◀○○○○○
CARBOHYDRATES	○○○○○○○○
PROTEIN & DAIRY	○○○○○○○
FATS	○○○○●

PER SERVING	
calories	68
kilojoules	285
protein	1 g
carbohydrate	8 g
total fat	4 g
saturated fat	1 g
monounsaturated fat	2 g
cholesterol	3 mg
sodium	261 mg
fiber	2 g

If the beet greens are still attached, cut them off, leaving about 1 inch (2.5 cm) of the stem intact. In a large pot fitted with a steamer basket, bring 1 inch water to a boil. Add the unpeeled beets, cover, and steam until tender, 20–25 minutes. Remove from the pot and let stand until cool enough to handle, then peel and cut into quarters. Set aside and keep warm.

Check the pot, add water to a depth of 1 inch if necessary, and return to a boil. Add the baby carrots, cover, and steam until tender, 5–7 minutes. (If the carrots are varied sizes, cut the larger ones into halves or thirds for even cooking.) Remove from the pot.

In a large bowl, toss the carrots with the butter, olive oil, lemon juice, and chopped dill. Add the beets, toss gently to combine, and transfer to a serving dish. Serve immediately, garnished with the dill sprigs.

1 lb (500 g) red and yellow baby beets, about 1½ inches (4 cm) in diameter

½ lb (250 g) baby carrots, peeled

2 teaspoons butter

1 tablespoon extra-virgin olive oil

1½ teaspoons fresh lemon juice

2 teaspoons chopped fresh dill, plus sprigs for garnish

Green Beans
with Red Pepper and Garlic

Green beans, also known as string beans or snap beans, are available year-round. To preserve their fresh flavor and texture, parboil the beans, immerse them in ice water to set their color, then sauté briefly.

SERVES 6

1 lb (500 g) green beans, stems trimmed

2 teaspoons olive oil

1 red bell pepper (capsicum), seeded and cut into julienne

½ teaspoon chile paste or red pepper flakes

1 clove garlic, finely chopped

1 teaspoon sesame oil

½ teaspoon salt

¼ teaspoon freshly ground black pepper

Cut the beans into 2-inch (5-cm) pieces. Bring a large saucepan three-fourths full of water to a boil. Add the beans and cook until they turn bright green and are tender-crisp, 1–3 minutes. Drain the beans, then plunge them into a bowl of ice water to stop the cooking. Drain again and set aside.

In a large frying pan, heat the olive oil over medium heat. Add the bell pepper and toss and stir for about 1 minute. Add the beans and sauté for 1 minute longer. Add the chile paste and garlic and toss and stir for 1 minute longer. The beans will be tender and bright green. Drizzle with the sesame oil and season with the salt and black pepper. Serve immediately.

Pyramid Servings

VEGETABLES	◀○○○●●
FRUITS	◀○○○○
CARBOHYDRATES	○○○○○○○○○
PROTEIN & DAIRY	○○○○○○○
FATS	○○○○○

PER SERVING	
calories	50
kilojoules	210
protein	2 g
carbohydrate	7 g
total fat	2 g
saturated fat	<1 g
monounsaturated fat	1 g
cholesterol	0 mg
sodium	201 mg
fiber	3 g

Warm Potato Salad

A mixture of smooth and whole-grain mustards forms the base for a vinaigrette much lighter than traditional mayonnaise dressings. This salad is most flavorful when served warm or at room temperature.

SERVES 6

1 lb (500 g) small red or white new potatoes (about 1½ inches/4 cm in diameter)

1 tablespoon Dijon mustard

1 tablespoon whole-grain mustard

2 tablespoons rice vinegar

2 teaspoons red wine vinegar or sherry vinegar

2 tablespoons minced shallot

4 teaspoons extra-virgin olive oil

2 tablespoons chopped fresh flat-leaf (Italian) parsley

¼ teaspoon salt

¼ teaspoon freshly ground pepper

Put the potatoes in a saucepan, add water to cover, and bring to a boil over high heat. Reduce the heat to medium and cook, uncovered, until the potatoes are tender, 15–20 minutes. Drain and let stand until just cool enough to handle. Cut each potato in half (or quarters, if the potatoes are large) and place in a warmed serving dish.

In a small bowl, whisk together the mustards, the vinegars, and the shallot until well blended. While whisking, slowly drizzle in the olive oil to make a thick dressing. Stir in the parsley, salt, and pepper. Pour the dressing over the warm potatoes, mix gently, and serve immediately.

Pyramid Servings

VEGETABLES	◀○○○○○
FRUITS	◀○○○○○
CARBOHYDRATES	○○○○○○●
PROTEIN & DAIRY	○○○○○○○
FATS	○○○○●

PER SERVING	
calories	89
kilojoules	372
protein	3 g
carbohydrate	15 g
total fat	3 g
saturated fat	0 g
monounsaturated fat	2 g
cholesterol	0 mg
sodium	202 mg
fiber	2 g

Asparagus
with Hazelnut Gremolata

SERVES 4

Gremolata, a mixture of chopped parsley, lemon zest, and garlic, here includes freshly toasted hazelnuts as well. This aromatic blend also complements steamed green beans, broccoli, and brussels sprouts.

Pyramid Servings

VEGETABLES	◀○○○○●
FRUITS	◀○○○○○
CARBOHYDRATES	○○○○○○○○
PROTEIN & DAIRY	○○○○○○○
FATS	○○○○○

PER SERVING	
calories	37
kilojoules	155
protein	2 g
carbohydrate	3 g
total fat	2 g
saturated fat	0 g
monounsaturated fat	2 g
cholesterol	0 mg
sodium	154 mg
fiber	1 g

In a large pot fitted with a steamer basket, bring about 1 inch (2.5 cm) water to a boil. Add the asparagus, cover, and steam until tender-crisp, about 4 minutes. Remove from the pot.

In a large bowl, combine the asparagus, garlic, chopped parsley, hazelnuts, the ¼ teaspoon lemon zest, the lemon juice, the olive oil, and the salt. Toss well to mix and coat.

Arrange the asparagus neatly on a serving platter and garnish with parsley sprigs and lemon zest. Serve immediately.

1 lb (500 g) asparagus, tough ends removed, then peeled if skin seems thick

1 clove garlic, minced

1 tablespoon chopped fresh flat-leaf (Italian) parsley, plus sprigs for garnish

1 tablespoon finely chopped toasted (page 138) hazelnuts (filberts)

¼ teaspoon finely grated lemon zest, plus extra for garnish

2 teaspoons fresh lemon juice

1 teaspoon extra-virgin olive oil

¼ teaspoon salt

Roasted Root Vegetables with Cumin and Coriander

The secret to perfect roasting is a hot oven and a pan large enough to eliminate crowding. This ensures a crisp, evenly browned exterior. Be sure to cut the vegetables to a uniform size for even cooking.

½ lb (250 g) sweet potatoes, peeled and cut into 1-inch (2.5-cm) pieces

½ lb (250 g) parsnips, peeled and cut into 1-inch (2.5-cm) pieces

½ lb (250 g) rutabagas, peeled and cut into 1-inch (2.5-cm) pieces

½ lb (250 g) turnips, peeled and cut into 1-inch (2.5-cm) pieces

2 tablespoons olive oil

1 teaspoon ground cumin

1 teaspoon ground coriander

½ teaspoon salt

¼ teaspoon freshly ground pepper

2 tablespoons chopped fresh cilantro (fresh coriander)

Position a rack in the lower third of the oven and preheat to 400°F (200°C).

In a large bowl, combine the vegetables, olive oil, cumin, ground coriander, and salt. Toss well to coat. Arrange the vegetables in a single layer on a large baking sheet.

Roast, stirring or shaking the vegetables every 15 minutes, until tender and evenly browned, about 45 minutes. Sprinkle with the pepper; taste and adjust the seasoning.

Transfer to a serving dish and sprinkle with the cilantro. Serve hot or at room temperature.

SERVES 8

Pyramid Servings

VEGETABLES	◀○○○○○
FRUITS	◀○○○○○
CARBOHYDRATES	○○○○○○○●
PROTEIN & DAIRY	○○○○○○○○
FATS	○○○○●

PER SERVING	
calories	101
kilojoules	423
protein	2 g
carbohydrate	16 g
total fat	4 g
saturated fat	1 g
monounsaturated fat	3 g
cholesterol	0 mg
sodium	179 mg
fiber	4 g

Pan-Braised Onions with Rosemary

Slow cooking brings out the sweetness of yellow onions in this rustic dish, while balsamic vinegar adds depth. The recipe can also be doubled. Make ahead or serve hot with roasted chicken.

Pyramid Servings

VEGETABLES	◀○●●●●
FRUITS	◀○○○○○
CARBOHYDRATES	○○○○○○○○○
PROTEIN & DAIRY	○○○○○○○○
FATS	○○○○●

PER SERVING	
calories	148
kilojoules	582
protein	3 g
carbohydrate	25 g
total fat	4 g
saturated fat	<1 g
monounsaturated fat	3 g
cholesterol	0 mg
sodium	190 mg
fiber	4 g

In a large, nonstick sauté or frying pan, heat the olive oil over medium-high heat. Add the onions, minced rosemary, and bay leaf. Reduce the heat to very low, cover tightly, and cook, stirring occasionally, until the onions are tender and beginning to turn golden, about 30 minutes. If the onions begin to stick at any point during the slow cooking, add a few tablespoons of water.

Add the vegetable stock to the pan and bring to a simmer. Cook until the stock evaporates completely, about 5 minutes. Add the vinegar and simmer until the liquid is completely absorbed, about 5 minutes longer. Season with the salt and pepper.

Transfer to a warmed serving dish and garnish with the rosemary sprigs. Serve immediately.

1 tablespoon extra-virgin olive oil

2 lb (1 kg) yellow onions, halved lengthwise and cut crosswise into slices ¼ inch (6 mm) thick

2 teaspoons minced fresh rosemary, plus sprigs for garnish

1 bay leaf

¼ cup (2 fl oz/60 ml) vegetable stock (page 139), broth, or dry white wine

½ cup (4 fl oz/125 ml) balsamic vinegar

¼ teaspoon salt

½ teaspoon freshly ground pepper

Steamed Summer Squash
with Warm Leek Vinaigrette

When you can find them, miniature pattypan and other summer squash are an attractive substitute for full-sized crooknecks and zucchini. The leek vinaigrette is also delicious over grilled fish.

SERVES 6

2 yellow crookneck squash, about ½ lb (250 g) total weight

2 zucchini (courgettes), about ½ lb (250 g) total weight

FOR THE VINAIGRETTE

2 tablespoons extra-virgin olive oil

1 leek, including tender green top, finely chopped (about 1 cup/4 oz/125 g)

1 tablespoon vegetable stock (page 139) or broth

1 tablespoon rice vinegar

1 tablespoon fresh lemon juice

½ teaspoon salt

¼ teaspoon freshly ground pepper

Trim the stems from the crooknecks and zucchini. Halve lengthwise and then cut the halves crosswise on the diagonal into slices ½ inch (12 mm) thick. Set aside.

To make the vinaigrette, in a saucepan, heat the olive oil over medium heat. Add the leek and sauté until soft, 10–12 minutes. Remove from the heat and stir in the vegetable stock, vinegar, lemon juice, salt, and pepper. Cover and keep warm.

Meanwhile, in a large pot fitted with a steamer basket, bring 1 inch (2.5 cm) water to a boil. Add the yellow squash and zucchini, cover, and steam until tender, about 10 minutes.

Transfer the squash to a warmed serving dish. Add the vinaigrette and toss gently to mix. Serve immediately.

Pyramid Servings

VEGETABLES	◀○○○○●
FRUITS	◀○○○○○
CARBOHYDRATES	○○○○○○○○
PROTEIN & DAIRY	○○○○○○○
FATS	○○○○●

PER SERVING	
calories	63
kilojoules	264
protein	1 g
carbohydrate	5 g
total fat	5 g
saturated fat	1 g
monounsaturated fat	3 g
cholesterol	0 mg
sodium	200 mg
fiber	2 g

Two-Potato Gratin

The buttery flavor of Yukon gold potatoes contrasts nicely with the firm texture of sweet potatoes in this scalloped potato–style dish. Serve with roasted chicken, pork, or beef.

SERVES 6

1 clove garlic, halved

3½ teaspoons olive oil

3 Yukon gold or red-skinned potatoes, about 1¼ lb (625 g) total weight, peeled and cut into slices ⅛ inch (3 mm) thick

1 sweet potato, about ½ lb (250 g), peeled and cut into slices ⅛ inch (3 mm) thick

1 tablespoon butter, melted

½ teaspoon salt

¼ teaspoon freshly ground pepper

1¼ cups (10 fl oz/310 ml) nonfat milk

⅛ teaspoon ground nutmeg

1 slice (1 oz/30 g) whole-wheat (wholemeal) bread, torn into pieces

Preheat the oven to 425°F (220°C). Rub the cut sides of the garlic on the bottom and sides of a large gratin dish or shallow 1½-qt (1.5-l) baking dish. Lightly coat the bottom and sides of the dish with 1 teaspoon of the olive oil.

Arrange half of the white potato slices in a single layer in the bottom of the gratin dish; top with half of the sweet potato slices. Drizzle the melted butter over the potato mixture and sprinkle with ¼ teaspoon of the salt and ⅛ teaspoon of the pepper. Layer the remaining white potato slices over the seasoned potato mixture. Top with the remaining sweet potato slices, ¼ teaspoon salt, and ⅛ teaspoon pepper.

In a small saucepan over medium-low heat, combine the milk and nutmeg. Bring to a boil. Remove from the heat and pour evenly over the potato mixture.

In a food processor, process the bread until small crumbs form. Add the remaining 2½ teaspoons olive oil and pulse to blend. Sprinkle the bread crumb mixture evenly over the potatoes. Bake until the potatoes are tender, 45–50 minutes. Let stand for 5 minutes before serving.

Pyramid Servings

VEGETABLES ◀ ○ ○ ○ ○ ○
FRUITS ◀ ○ ○ ○ ○ ○
CARBOHYDRATES ○ ○ ○ ○ ○ ○ ● ●
PROTEIN & DAIRY ○ ○ ○ ○ ○ ○ ○
FATS ○ ○ ○ ○ ●

PER SERVING	
calories	174
kilojoules	728
protein	5 g
carbohydrate	31 g
total fat	5 g
saturated fat	2 g
monounsaturated fat	3 g
cholesterol	6 mg
sodium	271 mg
fiber	3 g

Garden Peas with Fresh Mint

SERVES 6

The natural sweetness of fresh peas requires little adornment. Here, a handful of chopped mint underscores their straight-from-the-garden appeal. You can also experiment with tarragon or other fresh herbs.

Pyramid Servings

VEGETABLES ◀○○○●●
FRUITS ◀○○○○○
CARBOHYDRATES ○○○○○○○○○
PROTEIN & DAIRY ○○○○○○○
FATS ○○○○●

PER SERVING	
calories	86
kilojoules	360
protein	4 g
carbohydrate	12 g
total fat	3 g
saturated fat	0 g
monounsaturated fat	2 g
cholesterol	0 mg
sodium	102 mg
fiber	2 g

In a large pot fitted with a steamer basket, bring about 1 inch (2.5 cm) water to a boil. Add the peas, cover, and steam, tossing once, until tender, about 4 minutes. Transfer the peas to a large bowl, and add the olive oil, mint, salt, and pepper. Toss to mix. Serve immediately.

Alternatively, sauté the peas. In a sauté pan, heat the olive oil over medium heat. Add the peas and cook, stirring occasionally, just until tender, about 3 minutes. Stir in the mint. Season with the salt and pepper. Serve immediately.

3 lb (1.5 kg) English peas, shelled (about 3 cups/ 15 oz/470 g), or 1 lb (500 g) frozen shelled peas, thawed

1 tablespoon extra-virgin olive oil

2 tablespoons chopped fresh mint

¼ teaspoon salt

½ teaspoon freshly ground pepper

Fruits

Each piece of fruit offers a chance to thrill your taste buds while also helping build your body's defenses.

Mixed Fresh Berries
with Ginger Sauce

Make a double batch of this spicy, sweet ginger sauce and refrigerate it for up to 3 days. Spoon it onto angel food cake or fresh melon. If you can't find red currants, use peach slices or strawberries.

SERVES 6

FOR THE SAUCE

4 cups (1 lb/500 g) strawberries, hulled and halved

¼ cup (2 fl oz/60 ml) fresh orange juice

3 tablespoons chopped crystallized ginger

½ teaspoon vanilla extract (essence)

2 cups (8 oz/250 g) blackberries

1 cup (4 oz/125 g) raspberries

1 cup (4 oz/125 g) fresh red currants

Fresh mint leaves for garnish

To make the sauce, in a blender or food processor, combine the strawberries, orange juice, ginger, and vanilla. Process just until blended. Pass the purée through a fine-mesh sieve placed over a small bowl, pressing on the solids with a spatula or the back of a wooden spoon to extract all the juice.

In a large bowl, toss together the blackberries, raspberries, and currants, mixing well. Transfer to a serving bowl or individual bowls. Spoon the ginger sauce over the berries and garnish with the mint. Serve immediately.

Pyramid Servings

VEGETABLES	◀○○○○○
FRUITS	◀○○○○●
CARBOHYDRATES	○○○○○○○○
PROTEIN & DAIRY	○○○○○○○
FATS	○○○○○

PER SERVING	
calories	82
kilojoules	343
protein	1 g
carbohydrate	20 g
total fat	0 g
saturated fat	0 g
monounsaturated fat	0 g
cholesterol	0 mg
sodium	2 mg
fiber	5 g

Orange Slices with Citrus Syrup

SERVES 4

Several orange flavors are combined here to add intensity and depth to fresh orange slices. If you prefer a nonalcoholic version, simply leave out the liqueur; the syrup will still be rich and satisfying.

Pyramid Servings

VEGETABLES	◀○○○○○
FRUITS	◀○○●●●
CARBOHYDRATES	○○○○○○○○
PROTEIN & DAIRY	○○○○○○○
FATS	○○○○○

PER SERVING	
calories	162
kilojoules	678
protein	2 g
carbohydrate	39 g
total fat	1 g
saturated fat	0 g
monounsaturated fat	0 g
cholesterol	0 mg
sodium	2 mg
fiber	4 g

Working with 1 orange at a time, cut a thin slice off the top and the bottom, exposing the flesh. Stand the orange upright and, using a sharp knife, thickly cut off the peel, following the contour of the fruit and removing all the white pith and membrane. Cut the orange crosswise into slices ½ inch (12 mm) thick. Transfer to a shallow non-aluminum bowl or dish. Repeat with the remaining oranges. Set aside.

In a small saucepan over medium-high heat, combine the julienned zest with water to cover. Bring to a boil and boil for 1 minute. Drain and plunge the zest into a bowl of cold water. Set aside.

To make the syrup, combine the orange juice and honey in a large saucepan over medium-high heat. Bring to a boil, stirring to dissolve the honey. Reduce the heat to medium-low and simmer, uncovered, until the mixture thickens to a light syrup, about 5 minutes. Drain the orange zest and add to the syrup. Cook until the zest is translucent, 3–5 minutes.

Pour the orange syrup mixture over the oranges. Cover and refrigerate until well chilled or for up to 3 hours.

To serve, divide the orange slices among individual plates. Pour the syrup and zest over the orange slices, dividing it evenly. Drizzle each serving with 1½ teaspoons of the orange liqueur, if using. Garnish with the mint and serve immediately.

4 oranges

Zest of 1 orange, cut into julienne 4 inches (10 cm) long and ⅛ inch (3 mm) wide

FOR THE SYRUP

1½ cups (12 fl oz/375 ml) fresh orange juice, strained

2 tablespoons dark honey

2 tablespoons orange liqueur such as Grand Marnier or Cointreau (optional)

4 fresh mint sprigs

Sautéed Bananas with Caramel Sauce

With a glaze of caramel sauce, this banana dish is a sweet ending to any meal. Rich-flavored walnut oil lends an exotic accent. Apple juice is a good substitute for the rum in a nonalcoholic version.

SERVES 6

FOR THE SAUCE

1 tablespoon butter

1 tablespoon walnut oil or canola oil

1 tablespoon honey

2 tablespoons firmly packed brown sugar

3 tablespoons 1-percent low-fat milk

1 tablespoon dark raisins or golden raisins (sultanas)

4 firm bananas, about 1 lb (500 g) total weight

½ teaspoon canola oil

2 tablespoons dark rum or apple juice

To make the sauce, in a small saucepan, melt the butter over medium heat. Whisk in the oil, honey, and brown sugar. Cook, stirring continuously, until the sugar is dissolved, about 3 minutes. Stir in the milk, 1 tablespoon at a time, and then cook, stirring continuously, until the sauce thickens slightly, about 3 minutes. Remove from the heat and stir in the raisins. Set aside and keep warm.

Peel the bananas, then cut each crosswise into 3 sections. Cut each section in half lengthwise.

Lightly coat a large nonstick frying pan with the canola oil and place over medium-high heat. Add the bananas and sauté until they begin to brown, 3–4 minutes. Transfer to a plate and keep warm.

Add the rum to the pan, bring to a boil, and deglaze the pan, stirring with a wooden spoon to scrape up any browned bits from the bottom of the pan. Cook until reduced by half, 30–45 seconds. Return the bananas to the pan to rewarm.

To serve, divide the bananas among individual bowls or plates. Drizzle with the warm sauce and serve immediately.

Pyramid Servings

VEGETABLES	◀ ○○○○○
FRUITS	◀ ○○○●●
CARBOHYDRATES	○○○○○○○
PROTEIN & DAIRY	○○○○○○○
FATS	○○○○●

PER SERVING	
calories	146
kilojoules	611
protein	1 g
carbohydrate	27 g
total fat	5 g
saturated fat	1 g
monounsaturated fat	1 g
cholesterol	5 mg
sodium	25 mg
fiber	3 g

Baked Apples
with Cherries and Almonds

SERVES 6

Any good baking apple, such as Golden Delicious, Rome, or Granny Smith, will hold its shape beautifully for this dish. Serve it as a light dessert, or alongside roasted pork or pork tenderloin.

Pyramid Servings

VEGETABLES	◀○○○○○
FRUITS	◀○○○●●
CARBOHYDRATES	○○○○○○○○
PROTEIN & DAIRY	○○○○○○○
FATS	○○○○●

PER SERVING	
calories	179
kilojoules	749
protein	2 g
carbohydrate	37 g
total fat	4 g
saturated fat	0 g
monounsaturated fat	2 g
cholesterol	0 mg
sodium	5 mg
fiber	5 g

Preheat the oven to 350°F (180°C).

In a small bowl, toss together the cherries, almonds, wheat germ, brown sugar, cinnamon, and nutmeg until all the ingredients are evenly distributed. Set aside.

The apples can be left unpeeled, if you like. To peel the apples in a decorative fashion, with a vegetable peeler or a small, sharp knife, remove the peel from each apple in a circular motion, skipping every other row so that rows of peel alternate with rows of apple flesh. Working from the stem end, core each apple, stopping ¾ inch (2 cm) from the bottom.

Divide the cherry mixture evenly among the apples, pressing the mixture gently into each cavity.

Arrange the apples upright in a heavy ovenproof frying pan or small baking dish just large enough to hold them. Pour the apple juice and water into the pan. Drizzle the honey and oil evenly over the apples, and cover the pan snugly with aluminum foil. Bake until the apples are tender when pierced with a knife, 50–60 minutes.

Transfer the apples to individual plates and drizzle with the pan juices. Serve warm or at room temperature.

⅓ cup (1½ oz/45 g) dried cherries, coarsely chopped

3 tablespoons chopped almonds

1 tablespoon wheat germ

1 tablespoon firmly packed brown sugar

½ teaspoon ground cinnamon

⅛ teaspoon ground nutmeg

6 small Golden Delicious apples, about 1¾ lb (875 g) total weight

½ cup (4 fl oz/125 ml) apple juice

¼ cup (2 fl oz/60 ml) water

2 tablespoons dark honey

2 teaspoons walnut oil or canola oil

Ambrosia with Coconut and Toasted Almonds

This Southern classic is pretty and refreshing for dessert or as a snack. The simplicity of its flavors demands the sweetest fruit you can find. Sprinklings of toasted almonds and coconut offer richness with little fat.

SERVES 8

½ cup (2½ oz/75 g) slivered almonds

½ cup (2 oz/60 g) unsweetened flaked coconut

1 small pineapple

5 oranges

2 red apples, cored and diced

1 banana, halved lengthwise, peeled, and sliced crosswise

2 tablespoons cream sherry

Fresh mint leaves for garnish

Preheat the oven to 325°F (165°C). Spread the almonds on a baking sheet and bake, stirring occasionally, until golden and fragrant, about 10 minutes. Transfer immediately to a plate to cool. Add the coconut to the sheet and bake, stirring often, until lightly browned, about 10 minutes. Transfer immediately to a plate to cool.

Cut off the crown of leaves and the base of the pineapple. Stand the pineapple upright and, using a large, sharp knife, pare off the skin, cutting downward just below the surface in long, vertical strips and leaving the small brown "eyes" on the fruit. Lay the pineapple on its side. Aligning the knife blade with the diagonal rows of eyes, cut a shallow furrow, following a spiral pattern around the pineapple, to remove all the eyes. Cut the pineapple crosswise into slices ¾ inch (2 cm) thick, and remove the core with a small, sharp knife or small cookie cutter. Cut into cubes and set aside.

Working with 1 orange at a time, cut a thin slice off the top and the bottom, exposing the flesh. Stand the orange upright and, using a sharp knife, thickly cut off the peel, following the contour of the fruit and removing all the white pith and membrane. Holding the orange over a bowl, carefully cut along both sides of each section to free it from the membrane. As you work, discard any seeds and let the sections fall into the bowl. Repeat with the remaining oranges.

In a large bowl, combine the pineapple, oranges, apples, banana, and sherry. Toss gently to mix well. Divide the fruit mixture evenly among individual bowls. Sprinkle evenly with the toasted almonds and coconut and garnish with the mint. Serve immediately.

Pyramid Servings

VEGETABLES	◀○○○○○
FRUITS	◀○○○●●
CARBOHYDRATES	○○○○○○○○
PROTEIN & DAIRY	○○○○○○○
FATS	○○○○●

PER SERVING	
calories	146
kilojoules	611
protein	2 g
carbohydrate	26 g
total fat	4 g
saturated fat	1 g
monounsaturated fat	1 g
cholesterol	0 mg
sodium	1 mg
fiber	4 g

Salads

Never before have markets offered such a variety of fresh greens rich with disease-fighting antioxidants.

Greek Salad

The simple flavors of this Mediterranean salad provide the perfect opportunity to showcase a fruity extra-virgin olive oil in a lemony dressing. For variety, try romaine (cos) lettuce instead of spinach.

SERVES **8**

FOR THE VINAIGRETTE

1 tablespoon red wine vinegar

1 tablespoon fresh lemon juice

2 teaspoons chopped fresh oregano or ¾ teaspoon dried oregano

½ teaspoon salt

¼ teaspoon freshly ground pepper

2½ tablespoons extra-virgin olive oil

1 large eggplant (aubergine), about 1½ lb (750 g), trimmed and cut into ½-inch (12-mm) cubes

1 lb (500 g) spinach, stemmed and torn into bite-sized pieces

1 English (hothouse) cucumber, peeled, seeded, and diced

1 tomato, seeded and diced

½ red onion, diced

2 tablespoons pitted, chopped black Greek olives

2 tablespoons crumbled feta cheese

Position a rack in the lower third of the oven and preheat to 450°F (230°C). Lightly coat a baking sheet with olive oil cooking spray.

To make the vinaigrette, in a small bowl, whisk together the vinegar, lemon juice, oregano, salt, and pepper. While whisking, slowly add the olive oil in a thin stream until emulsified. Set aside.

Spread the eggplant cubes in a single layer on the prepared baking sheet. Spray the eggplant with olive oil cooking spray. Roast for 10 minutes. Turn the cubes and roast until softened and lightly golden, 8–10 minutes longer. Set aside and let cool completely.

In a large bowl, combine the spinach, cucumber, tomato, onion, and cooled eggplant. Pour the vinaigrette over the salad and toss gently to mix well and coat evenly. Divide the salad among individual plates. Sprinkle with the olives and feta. Serve immediately.

Pyramid Servings

VEGETABLES	◀ ○○○●●
FRUITS	◀ ○○○○○
CARBOHYDRATES	○○○○○○○○
PROTEIN & DAIRY	○○○○○○○
FATS	○○○○●

PER SERVING	
calories	88
kilojoules	368
protein	3 g
carbohydrate	9 g
total fat	5 g
saturated fat	1 g
monounsaturated fat	3 g
cholesterol	2 mg
sodium	245 mg
fiber	3 g

Yellow Pear and Cherry Tomato Salad

SERVES 6

Ripe tomatoes, fresh basil, and olive oil always make a superb salad. But the combination looks especially spectacular when composed with brightly colored yellow pear, orange, and red cherry tomatoes.

Pyramid Servings

VEGETABLES	◀○○○○●
FRUITS	◀○○○○○
CARBOHYDRATES	○○○○○○○○
PROTEIN & DAIRY	○○○○○○○○
FATS	○○○○●

PER SERVING	
calories	47
kilojoules	197
protein	1 g
carbohydrate	6 g
total fat	3 g
saturated fat	0 g
monounsaturated fat	2 g
cholesterol	0 mg
sodium	108 mg
fiber	1 g

To make the vinaigrette, in a small bowl, combine the vinegar and shallot and let stand for 15 minutes. Add the olive oil, salt, and pepper and whisk until well blended.

In a large serving or salad bowl, toss together all the tomatoes. Pour the vinaigrette over the tomatoes, add the basil shreds, and toss gently to mix well and coat evenly. Serve immediately.

FOR THE VINAIGRETTE

2 tablespoons sherry vinegar or red wine vinegar

1 tablespoon minced shallot

1 tablespoon extra-virgin olive oil

¼ teaspoon salt

⅛ teaspoon freshly ground pepper

1½ cups (9 oz/280 g) yellow pear tomatoes, halved

1½ cups (9 oz/280 g) orange cherry tomatoes, halved

1½ cups (9 oz/280 g) red cherry tomatoes, halved

4 large fresh basil leaves, cut into chiffonade

Mesclun Salad with Radishes, Avocado, and Blood Oranges

The mix of gourmet salad greens called mesclun may include oakleaf lettuce, arugula (rocket), frisée, mizuna, mâche, radicchio, and sorrel. Here, it is brightened with the red flesh of blood oranges.

SERVES 6

2 small blood oranges or other oranges

1 tablespoon rice vinegar

½ teaspoon Dijon mustard

1 tablespoon extra-virgin olive oil

¼ teaspoon salt

¼ teaspoon freshly ground pepper

6 cups (6 oz/185 g) mesclun or mixed young salad greens

4 red radishes, trimmed and very thinly sliced

½ small avocado, peeled and thinly sliced

2 tablespoons crumbled blue cheese

Working with 1 orange at a time, cut a thin slice off the top and the bottom, exposing the flesh. Stand the orange upright and, using a sharp knive, thickly cut off the peel, following the contour of the fruit and removing all the white pith and membrane. Holding the orange over a small bowl, carefully cut along both sides of each section to free it from the membrane. As you work, discard any seeds and let the sections and any juice fall into the bowl. Repeat with the second orange. When both oranges are sectioned, squeeze the membranes into the bowl to extract all of the juice.

To make the vinaigrette, in a small bowl, whisk together 2 tablespoons of the captured blood orange juice, the vinegar, and the mustard. While whisking, slowly add the olive oil in a thin stream until emulsified. Whisk in the salt and pepper. Reserve any remaining orange juice for another use.

In a large bowl, combine the mesclun, radishes, and orange sections. Pour the vinaigrette over the salad and toss gently to mix well and coat evenly.

To serve, divide the salad among individual plates. Top each portion with slices of avocado and sprinkle with the crumbled cheese.

Pyramid Servings

VEGETABLES	◀○○○○●
FRUITS	◀○○○○●
CARBOHYDRATES	○○○○○○○○
PROTEIN & DAIRY	○○○○○○○
FATS	○○○○●

PER SERVING	
calories	105
kilojoules	439
protein	3 g
carbohydrate	14 g
total fat	5 g
saturated fat	1 g
monounsaturated fat	3 g
cholesterol	2 mg
sodium	170 mg
fiber	4 g

Warm Coleslaw
with Honey Dressing

Cabbage is one of the healthful cruciferous vegetables. For this slaw, sliced vegetables are quickly stir-fried, then tossed in a hot dressing. Serve with Mahimahi with Macadamia Nut Crust (page 109).

SERVES 6

6 teaspoons olive oil

1 yellow onion, finely chopped

1 teaspoon dry mustard

1 large carrot, peeled and cut into julienne

½ head napa cabbage, cored and thinly sliced crosswise (about 5 cups/14 oz/440 g)

3 tablespoons cider vinegar

1 tablespoon dark honey

½ teaspoon salt

¼ teaspoon freshly ground pepper

½ teaspoon caraway seed

1 tablespoon chopped fresh flat-leaf (Italian) parsley

In a large nonstick sauté pan, heat 2 teaspoons of the olive oil over medium-high heat until hot but not smoking. Add the onion and mustard and sauté until the onion is soft and lightly golden, about 6 minutes. Transfer to a large bowl.

Reduce the heat to medium and add 2 more teaspoons of the olive oil to the pan. Add the carrot and toss and stir constantly until the carrot is tender-crisp, about 3 minutes. Transfer to the bowl with the onion.

Add the remaining 2 teaspoons oil to the pan over medium heat. Add the cabbage and toss and stir constantly until the cabbage just begins to wilt, about 3 minutes. Quickly transfer the cabbage to the bowl with the other vegetables.

Quickly add the vinegar and honey to the pan over medium heat, stirring until combined and bubbly and the honey is dissolved. Pour over the slaw. Add the salt and pepper and toss well. Garnish with the caraway seed and parsley and serve warm.

Pyramid Servings

VEGETABLES	◀︎○○○●●
FRUITS	◀︎○○○○○
CARBOHYDRATES	○○○○○○○○
PROTEIN & DAIRY	○○○○○○○
FATS	○○○○●

PER SERVING	
calories	91
kilojoules	381
protein	2 g
carbohydrate	12 g
total fat	5 g
saturated fat	<1 g
monounsaturated fat	3 g
cholesterol	0 mg
sodium	221 mg
fiber	3 g

Soups

Soup can span a daily menu's whole spectrum, from quick lunch to light side dish to hearty dinner.

Curried Carrot Soup, page 74

Summer Vegetable Soup

SERVES **8**

The midsummer wealth of vegetables and herbs makes it a pleasure to prepare this satisfying soup. Despite the bountiful ingredients, the soup is quick to make. For a heartier version, add shredded chicken.

Pyramid Servings

VEGETABLES	◄ ○○○●●
FRUITS	◄ ○○○○○
CARBOHYDRATES	○○○○○○○○○
PROTEIN & DAIRY	○○○○○○○○○
FATS	○○○○○

PER SERVING	
calories	60
kilojoules	251
protein	2 g
carbohydrate	9 g
total fat	2 g
saturated fat	<1 g
monounsaturated fat	1 g
cholesterol	0 mg
sodium	311 mg
fiber	2 g

In a large saucepan, heat the olive oil over medium heat. Add the onion and sauté until soft and translucent, about 4 minutes. Add the garlic and sauté for 30 seconds; do not let the garlic brown. Add the tomatoes, oregano, and cumin and sauté until the tomatoes are softened, about 4 minutes.

Add the stock and the bay leaf and bring to a boil, then reduce the heat to medium-low and bring to a simmer. Add the carrot and bell pepper and cook for 2 minutes. Add the zucchini and simmer until the vegetables are tender, about 3 minutes longer. Stir in the grated lemon zest and cilantro. Season with the salt and pepper. Discard the bay leaf.

Ladle the soup into individual bowls or mugs and serve immediately.

1 tablespoon olive oil

1 yellow onion, chopped

3 cloves garlic, chopped

4 plum (Roma) tomatoes, peeled and seeded (page 137), then diced

1 tablespoon chopped fresh oregano or 1 teaspoon dried oregano

1 teaspoon ground cumin

4 cups (32 fl oz/1 l) vegetable stock (page 139) or broth

1 bay leaf

1 carrot, peeled, halved lengthwise, and thinly sliced crosswise

1 yellow bell pepper (capsicum), seeded and diced

1 zucchini (courgette), halved lengthwise and thinly sliced crosswise

1 tablespoon grated lemon zest

2 tablespoons chopped fresh cilantro (fresh coriander)

¼ teaspoon salt

¼ teaspoon freshly ground pepper

Split Pea Soup

When you want a quick, hearty meal, this soup, made with yellow split peas, pairs well with crusty whole-grain bread or a fresh-vegetable medley. Or serve it with Warm Coleslaw with Honey Dressing (page 67).

SERVES 4

FOR THE CHIVE CREAM

3 tablespoons coarsely chopped fresh chives, plus long cuts for garnish

3 tablespoons nonfat plain yogurt

1 tablespoon low-fat buttermilk

¼ teaspoon sugar

Pinch of salt

2 tablespoons olive oil

1 yellow onion, chopped

½ teaspoon salt

1 large carrot, peeled and chopped

2 cloves garlic, minced

1½ cups (10½ oz/330 g) dried yellow or green split peas, picked over, rinsed, and drained

3 cups (24 fl oz/750 ml) water

3 cups (24 fl oz/750 ml) vegetable stock (page 139) or broth

¼ teaspoon freshly ground pepper

½ cup (30 oz/90 g) chopped lean ham

To make the chive cream, in a small blender or food processor, combine the chopped chives, yogurt, buttermilk, sugar, and the pinch of salt. Process until well blended. Cover and refrigerate until needed.

In a large saucepan, heat the olive oil over medium heat. Add the onion and sauté until soft and lightly golden, about 6 minutes. Stir in ¼ teaspoon of the salt. Add the carrot and sauté until the carrot is softened, about 5 minutes. Add the garlic and sauté for 1 minute. Stir in the split peas, water, stock, the remaining ¼ teaspoon salt, and the pepper and bring to a boil. Reduce the heat to low, cover partially, and simmer until the peas are tender, 60–65 minutes.

In a blender or food processor, purée the soup in batches until smooth and return to the saucepan over medium heat. Reheat gently.

Ladle into warmed individual bowls. Top each serving with a drizzle or swirl of chive cream and garnish with a sprinkle of chopped ham and a few long cuts of fresh chives. Serve immediately.

Pyramid Servings

VEGETABLES	◀○○○●●
FRUITS	◀○○○○○
CARBOHYDRATES	○○○○○○○○○
PROTEIN & DAIRY	○○○○●●●
FATS	○○○○○

PER SERVING	
calories	393
kilojoules	1,644
protein	23 g
carbohydrate	56 g
total fat	11 g
saturated fat	1 g
monounsaturated fat	6 g
cholesterol	7 mg
sodium	695 mg
fiber	12 g

Curried Carrot Soup

A splash of lime juice and a blend of spices transform an everyday carrot soup into a sophisticated indulgence. Accompany the soup with a green salad and crusty whole-grain bread for a complete meal.

Pyramid Servings

VEGETABLES	◀○○○●●
FRUITS	◀○○○○○
CARBOHYDRATES	○○○○○○○○
PROTEIN & DAIRY	○○○○○○○
FATS	○○○○●

PER SERVING	
calories	80
kilojoules	335
protein	6 g
carbohydrate	5 g
total fat	4 g
saturated fat	1 g
monounsaturated fat	2 g
cholesterol	3 mg
sodium	147 mg
fiber	1 g

In a large saucepan, heat the olive oil over medium heat. Add the mustard seed. When the seeds just start to pop, after about 1 minute, add the onion and sauté until soft and translucent, about 4 minutes. Add the carrots, ginger, jalapeño, and curry powder and sauté until the seasonings are fragrant, about 3 minutes.

Add 3 cups (24 fl oz/750 ml) of the stock, raise the heat to high, and bring to a boil. Reduce the heat to medium-low and simmer, uncovered, until the carrots are tender, about 6 minutes.

In a blender or food processor, purée the soup in batches until smooth and return to the saucepan. Stir in the remaining 2 cups (16 fl oz/500 ml) stock. Return the soup to medium heat and reheat gently. Just before serving, stir in the chopped cilantro and lime juice. Season with the salt, if desired.

Ladle into warmed individual bowls. Garnish with yogurt, lime zest, and cilantro leaves.

1 tablespoon olive oil

1 teaspoon mustard seed

½ yellow onion, chopped

1 lb (500 g) carrots, peeled and cut into ½-inch (12-mm) pieces

1 tablespoon plus 1 teaspoon peeled and chopped fresh ginger

½ jalapeño chile, seeded

2 teaspoons curry powder

5 cups (40 fl oz/1.25 l) chicken stock, vegetable stock (page 139), or broth

¼ cup (⅓ oz/10 g) chopped fresh cilantro (fresh coriander), plus leaves for garnish

2 tablespoons fresh lime juice

½ teaspoon salt (optional)

3 tablespoons nonfat plain yogurt or low-fat sour cream

Grated zest of 1 lime

Fresh Tomato Soup
with Crispy Herb Toasts

When fresh tomatoes are at their peak, their intense flavor makes this soup a treat. Serve it with grilled vegetables for a light summer lunch or supper. In winter, substitute vine-ripened hothouse tomatoes.

SERVES 4

8 slices whole-grain baguette, ½ inch (12 mm) thick

1 tablespoon chopped fresh basil

2 teaspoons chopped fresh oregano

4 teaspoons grated Parmesan cheese

4 tomatoes

2 teaspoons olive oil

½ small yellow onion, diced

1 tablespoon tomato paste

1½ cups (12 fl oz/375 ml) 1-percent low-fat milk

½ teaspoon salt

⅛ teaspoon freshly ground pepper

Preheat the broiler (grill). Arrange the baguette slices on a broiler pan and top each slice with a sprinkling of basil, oregano, and cheese. Place about 4 inches (10 cm) from the heat source and broil (grill) until the cheese is melted, 45–60 seconds. Watch carefully to prevent burning. Set the herb toasts aside.

Peel and seed the tomatoes (page 137), then cut them into a neat dice. In a large, heavy saucepan, heat the olive oil over medium heat. Add the onion and sauté until soft and translucent, about 4 minutes. Add the tomatoes and tomato paste and bring to a boil. Reduce the heat to medium-low and simmer, uncovered, until the soup thickens, 20–25 minutes.

In a blender or food processor, purée the soup in batches until smooth and return to the pan. Stir in the milk, salt, and pepper and reheat gently. Ladle into individual bowls, garnish each with 2 herb toasts, and serve.

Pyramid Servings

VEGETABLES	◀○○○○●
FRUITS	◀○○○○○
CARBOHYDRATES	○○○○○○○●
PROTEIN & DAIRY	○○○○○○●
FATS	○○○○○

PER SERVING	
calories	188
kilojoules	787
protein	8 g
carbohydrate	28 g
total fat	6 g
saturated fat	2 g
monounsaturated fat	3 g
cholesterol	5 mg
sodium	487 mg
fiber	4 g

Pasta & Grains

Grains are the soul of many meals,
from cereal to sandwiches to pasta,
but it's whole grains that we need.

Spinach Lasagne
with Sun-Dried Tomato Sauce

This hearty main dish can be prepared ahead, refrigerated, and baked later. Add the time-saving "no-boil" noodles directly to the dish. Alternatively, cook ¾ pound (375 g) regular spinach lasagne sheets.

SERVES **8**

2 tablespoons plus
   2 teaspoons olive oil

1½ tablespoons all-
   purpose (plain) flour

2 cloves garlic, minced

1 cup (8 fl oz/250 ml) plain
   soy milk (soya milk)

1 cup (8 fl oz/250 ml) vegetable stock (page 139)

2 green (spring) onions,
   sliced

½ cup (4 oz/125 g) dry-
   packed sun-dried toma-
   toes, soaked in water,
   drained, and chopped

10 oz (315 g) fresh cremini
   mushrooms, sliced

1 shallot, minced

1 tablespoon chopped
   fresh parsley

¼ teaspoon salt

6 cups (12 oz/375 g) baby
   spinach leaves, chopped

2 cups (16 oz/500 g) nonfat
   ricotta cheese

¾ cup (3 oz/90 g) grated
   Parmesan cheese

1 egg white

12 no-boil spinach lasagne
   sheets, about 7 by 3½
   inches (18 by 9 cm)

1 tablespoon chopped
   fresh basil

In a saucepan, heat 2 tablespoons olive oil over medium-high heat. Whisk in the flour and cook for 1–2 minutes, stirring constantly. Add the garlic and continue to whisk until the garlic is fragrant, about 30 seconds. Whisk in the soy milk and stock all at once. Cook and stir until slightly thickened. Remove from the heat and stir in the green onions and sun-dried tomatoes. Set the sauce aside.

In a large nonstick frying pan, heat 1 teaspoon of the olive oil over medium-high heat. Add the mushrooms and shallot and sauté until lightly browned, about 10 minutes. Stir in the parsley and salt. Transfer to a bowl and set aside.

In the same pan, heat the remaining 1 teaspoon olive oil over medium-high heat. Add the spinach and stir quickly until the spinach is wilted but still bright green. Remove from the heat. Let cool slightly. In a large bowl, beat together the ricotta, ½ cup (2 oz/60 g) of the Parmesan, and the egg white. Stir in the spinach and set aside.

Preheat the oven to 375°F (190°C). Lightly coat a 9-by-13-inch (23-by-33-cm) baking dish with cooking spray. Spread ½ cup (4 fl oz/125 ml) of the sauce in the dish and cover with 3 sheets of the pasta. Spoon half of the spinach mixture onto the pasta and spread gently. Cover with 3 more pasta sheets. Top with another ½ cup of sauce. Spread the mushroom mixture on top and cover with another ½ cup of sauce, then a layer of pasta. Spoon in the remaining spinach filling and top with the last 3 pasta sheets. Add the remaining sauce and the remaining ¼ cup (1 oz/30 g) Parmesan. Cover loosely with foil and bake for 25 minutes. Remove the foil and bake until golden, about 10 minutes longer. Let stand for 10 minutes before serving. Garnish with the basil.

Pyramid Servings

VEGETABLES	◀○○●●●
FRUITS	◀○○○○○
CARBOHYDRATES	○○○○○○○●
PROTEIN & DAIRY	○○○○○○●
FATS	○○○○●

PER SERVING	
calories	288
kilojoules	803
protein	17 g
carbohydrate	39 g
total fat	8 g
saturated fat	2 g
monounsaturated fat	4 g
cholesterol	6 mg
sodium	526 mg
fiber	4 g

Orzo with Cherry Tomatoes, Capers, and Lemon

This simple pasta dish lends itself to variation. Try it with different herbs, add slivers of spinach, or replace the tomatoes with sautéed mushrooms. Orzo is a rice-shaped pasta that readily absorbs flavors.

SERVES 4

2 teaspoons extra-virgin olive oil

2 cups (12 oz/375 g) cherry tomatoes, halved

1 clove garlic, minced

1 cup (7 oz/220 g) orzo

2 cups (16 fl oz/500 ml) chicken stock, vegetable stock (page 139), or broth

2 teaspoons chopped fresh thyme

2 teaspoons capers, drained and finely chopped

1 tablespoon pine nuts, finely chopped

1 tablespoon grated Parmesan cheese

1 tablespoon grated lemon zest

¼ teaspoon salt

¼ teaspoon freshly ground pepper

In a frying pan, heat the olive oil over medium heat. Add the tomatoes and garlic and cook until the tomatoes are tender, about 3 minutes. Set aside.

In a large saucepan, combine the orzo and chicken stock over medium-high heat. Bring to a boil, then reduce the heat to low, cover, and simmer until the pasta is al dente, about 7 minutes. Remove from the heat and let stand, covered, until almost all of the liquid is absorbed, about 3 minutes.

Add the thyme, capers, pine nuts, cheese, lemon zest, salt, and pepper and toss gently to mix. Add the tomato mixture and toss until all the ingredients are evenly distributed. Spoon the pasta into warmed individual bowls and serve immediately.

Pyramid Servings

VEGETABLES	◀○○●●●
FRUITS	◀○○○○○
CARBOHYDRATES	○○○○○○●●
PROTEIN & DAIRY	○○○○○○○
FATS	○○○○●

PER SERVING	
calories	215
kilojoules	900
protein	9 g
carbohydrate	38 g
total fat	5 g
saturated fat	<1 g
monounsaturated fat	1 g
cholesterol	1 mg
sodium	295 mg
fiber	2 g

Double-Corn Spoon Bread

SERVES 8

Spoon bread is made from cornmeal that is cooked on the stove top before whipped eggs are folded in. It is then cooked again, in the oven, like a soufflé. In this light version, only the egg whites are used.

Pyramid Servings

VEGETABLES	◀○○○○○
FRUITS	◀○○○○○
CARBOHYDRATES	○○○○○○○●
PROTEIN & DAIRY	○○○○○○●
FATS	○○○○○

PER SERVING	
calories	159
kilojoules	665
protein	7 g
carbohydrate	22 g
total fat	5 g
saturated fat	<1 g
monounsaturated fat	3 g
cholesterol	1 mg
sodium	300 mg
fiber	3 g

Preheat the oven to 375°F (190°C). Lightly coat a 3-qt (3-l) soufflé dish with olive oil cooking spray.

In a saucepan over medium heat, combine the soy milk, stock, olive oil, and honey. Heat until very hot but not boiling. Reduce the heat to low so the mixture simmers. Add the cornmeal in a stream while whisking constantly. Cook, stirring constantly, until the mixture thickens, about 5 minutes. Transfer to a large bowl. Add the corn kernels, shallot, thyme, baking powder, and salt and stir to combine.

In a large, spotlessly clean bowl, using an electric mixer on high speed, beat the egg whites until stiff peaks form. Gently whisk one-third of the whites into the cornmeal mixture to lighten it. Using a rubber spatula, gently fold the remaining egg whites into the batter, mixing just until incorporated.

Pour the batter into the prepared soufflé dish and sprinkle with the cheese. Bake until puffed and lightly golden, about 35 minutes. Let stand in the dish for 5 minutes before serving. Serve hot.

2 cups (16 fl oz/500 ml) plain soy milk (soya milk)

2 cups (16 fl oz/500 ml) chicken stock, vegetable stock (page 139), or broth

3 tablespoons olive oil

1 tablespoon dark honey

1 cup (5 oz/155 g) corn-meal, preferably stone-ground

1¼ cups (7½ oz/235 g) fresh corn kernels (cut from 2 or 3 ears corn)

1 tablespoon minced shallot

1 tablespoon chopped fresh thyme

1 teaspoon baking powder

½ teaspoon salt

4 egg whites

1 tablespoon grated Parmesan cheese

Brown Rice Pilaf

SERVES **8**

Any brown rice will work in this recipe, but darker-toned Wehani looks particularly good. Invest in the pistachio oil if you can. Its flavor is so intense that just a bit makes this light side dish taste incredibly rich.

Pyramid Servings

VEGETABLES	◀○○○○○
FRUITS	◀○○○○●
CARBOHYDRATES	○○○○○○○●
PROTEIN & DAIRY	○○○○○○○
FATS	○○○○●

PER SERVING	
calories	156
kilojoules	653
protein	3 g
carbohydrate	25 g
total fat	5 g
saturated fat	1 g
monounsaturated fat	2 g
cholesterol	0 mg
sodium	221 mg
fiber	2 g

In a saucepan over high heat, combine the rice, water, ¼ teaspoon of the salt, and the saffron. Bring to a boil. Reduce the heat to low, cover, and simmer until the water is absorbed and the rice is tender, about 45 minutes. Transfer to a large bowl and keep warm.

In a small bowl, combine the orange zest and juice, pistachio oil, and the remaining ½ teaspoon salt. Whisk to blend. Pour the orange mixture over the warm rice. Add the nuts and apricots and toss gently to mix and coat. Serve immediately.

1⅛ cups (8 oz/250 g) dark brown rice, rinsed and drained

2 cups (16 fl oz/500 ml) water

¾ teaspoon salt

¼ teaspoon saffron threads or ground turmeric

½ teaspoon grated orange zest

3 tablespoons fresh orange juice

1½ tablespoons pistachio oil or canola oil

¼ cup (1 oz/30g) chopped pistachio nuts

¼ cup (1½ oz/45 g) dried apricots, chopped

Savory Buckwheat Pilaf with Toasted Spices

Similar to rice pilaf, this richly flavored side dish features buckwheat groats plumped up in simmering vegetable stock and seasoned with fresh herbs and pungent spices.

SERVES 6

1 tablespoon olive oil

1 yellow onion, chopped

1 cup (8 oz/250 g) buck-wheat groats

3 cloves garlic, minced

½ teaspoon cumin seed

½ teaspoon mustard seed

¼ teaspoon ground cardamom

2 cups (16 fl oz/500 ml) vegetable stock (page 139) or broth

1 tomato, peeled and seeded (page 137), then diced

½ teaspoon salt

2 tablespoons chopped fresh cilantro (fresh coriander)

In a saucepan, heat the olive oil over medium heat. Add the onion and sauté until soft and translucent, about 4 minutes. Add the buckwheat groats, garlic, cumin seed, mustard seed, and cardamom. Sauté, stirring constantly, until the spices and garlic are fragrant and the buckwheat is lightly toasted, about 3 minutes.

Carefully pour in the stock. Bring to a boil, then reduce the heat to medium-low, cover, and simmer until the liquid is absorbed, about 10 minutes. Remove from the heat and let stand, covered, for 2 minutes.

Stir in the tomato and salt. Transfer to a serving bowl and sprinkle with the cilantro. Serve immediately.

Pyramid Servings

VEGETABLES	◀○○○○●
FRUITS	◀○○○○○
CARBOHYDRATES	○○○○○○○●
PROTEIN & DAIRY	○○○○○○○
FATS	○○○○●

PER SERVING	
calories	139
kilojoules	582
protein	4 g
carbohydrate	25 g
total fat	3 g
saturated fat	<1 g
monounsaturated fat	2 g
cholesterol	0 mg
sodium	198 mg
fiber	3 g

Banana-Oatmeal Hotcakes with Spiced Maple Syrup

Mashed bananas and cooked oats help keep these pancakes moist and flavorful. If you don't love syrup, warm some sliced bananas in a frying pan with a small amount of butter or oil and spoon them on top.

SERVES 6

½ cup (5½ oz/170 g) maple syrup

½ cinnamon stick

3 whole cloves

½ cup (1½ oz/45 g) old-fashioned rolled oats

1 cup (8 fl oz/250 ml) water

2 tablespoons firmly packed light brown sugar

2 tablespoons canola oil

½ cup (2½ oz/75 g) whole-wheat (wholemeal) flour

½ cup (2½ oz/75 g) all-purpose (plain) flour

1½ teaspoons baking powder

¼ teaspoon baking soda (bicarbonate of soda)

¼ teaspoon salt

¼ teaspoon ground cinnamon

½ cup (4 fl oz/125 ml) 1-percent low-fat milk

¼ cup (2 oz/60 g) nonfat plain yogurt

1 banana, peeled and mashed

1 egg, lightly beaten

In a small saucepan, combine the maple syrup, cinnamon stick, and cloves. Place over medium heat and bring to a boil. Remove from the heat and let steep for 15 minutes. Remove the cinnamon stick and cloves with a slotted spoon. Set the syrup aside and keep warm.

In a large microwave-safe bowl, combine the oats and water. Microwave on high until the oats are creamy and tender, about 3 minutes. Stir in the brown sugar and canola oil. Set aside to cool slightly.

In a bowl, combine the flours, baking powder, baking soda, salt, and ground cinnamon. Whisk to blend.

Add the milk, yogurt, and mashed banana to the oats and stir until well blended. Beat in the egg. Add the flour mixture to the oat mixture and stir just until moistened.

Place a nonstick frying pan or griddle over medium heat. When a drop of water sizzles as it hits the pan, spoon ¼ cup (2 fl oz/60 ml) pancake batter into the pan. Cook until the pancake's top surface is covered with bubbles and the edges are lightly browned, about 2 minutes. Turn and cook until the bottom is well browned and the pancake is cooked through, 1–2 minutes longer. Repeat with the remaining pancake batter.

Place the pancakes on warmed individual plates. Drizzle with the warm syrup and serve immediately.

Pyramid Servings

VEGETABLES	◀○○○○○
FRUITS	◀○○○○●
CARBOHYDRATES	○○○○○●●
PROTEIN & DAIRY	○○○○○○○
FATS	○○○○●

PER SERVING	
calories	268
kilojoules	1,121
protein	6 g
carbohydrate	48 g
total fat	6 g
saturated fat	1 g
monounsaturated fat	3 g
cholesterol	36 mg
sodium	230 mg
fiber	3 g

Three-Grain Raspberry Muffins

MAKES 12 MUFFINS

Cornmeal gives these muffins a crunchy texture that pairs well with any sweet berry, from raspberries to blueberries. If one dozen muffins sounds like too many, freeze any extras in a lock-top plastic bag.

Pyramid Servings

VEGETABLES	◀○○○○○
FRUITS	◀○○○○●
CARBOHYDRATES	○○○○○○○●
PROTEIN & DAIRY	○○○○○○○
FATS	○○○○●

PER MUFFIN	
calories	162
kilojoules	678
protein	3 g
carbohydrate	27 g
total fat	5 g
saturated fat	1 g
monounsaturated fat	3 g
cholesterol	19 mg
sodium	156 mg
fiber	2 g

Preheat the oven to 400°F (200°C). Line a 12-cup muffin pan with paper or foil liners.

In a large microwave-safe bowl, combine the oats and milk. Microwave on high until the oats are creamy and tender, about 3 minutes. Set aside.

In a large bowl, combine the flour, cornmeal, bran, baking powder, and salt. Whisk to blend. Add the honey, canola oil, lime zest, oats mixture, and egg. Beat just until moistened but still slightly lumpy. Gently fold in the raspberries.

Spoon the batter into the muffin cups, filling each cup about two-thirds full. Bake until the tops are golden brown and a toothpick inserted into the center of a muffin comes out clean, 16–18 minutes. Transfer the muffins to a wire rack and let cool completely.

½ cup (1½ oz/45 g) rolled oats

1 cup (8 fl oz/250 ml) 1-percent low-fat milk or plain soy milk (soya milk)

¾ cup (4 oz/125 g) all-purpose (plain) flour

½ cup (2½ oz/75 g) cornmeal, preferably stone-ground

¼ cup (½ oz/15 g) wheat bran

1 tablespoon baking powder

¼ teaspoon salt

½ cup (6 oz/185 g) dark honey

3½ tablespoons canola oil

2 teaspoons grated lime zest

1 egg, lightly beaten

⅔ cup (2½ oz/75 g) raspberries

Pumpkin-Hazelnut Tea Cake

If pumpkins are in season, roast a small pie pumpkin and purée the flesh in a blender or food processor for this loaf cake. Otherwise, use canned pumpkin. This cake makes a nice holiday gift.

3 tablespoons canola oil

¾ cup (6 oz/185 g) home-made or canned pumpkin purée

½ cup (6 oz/185 g) honey

3 tablespoons firmly packed brown sugar

2 eggs, lightly beaten

1 cup (5 oz/155 g) whole-wheat (wholemeal) flour

½ cup (2½ oz/75 g) all-purpose (plain) flour

2 tablespoons flaxseed

½ teaspoon baking powder

½ teaspoon ground allspice

½ teaspoon ground cinnamon

½ teaspoon ground nutmeg

¼ teaspoon ground cloves

¼ teaspoon salt

2 tablespoons chopped hazelnuts (filberts)

Preheat the oven to 350°F (180°C). Lightly coat an 8-by-4-inch (20-by-10-cm) loaf pan with cooking spray.

In a large bowl, using an electric mixer on low speed, beat together the canola oil, pumpkin purée, honey, brown sugar, and eggs until well blended.

In a small bowl, whisk together the flours, flaxseed, baking powder, allspice, cinnamon, nutmeg, cloves, and salt. Add the flour mixture to the pumpkin mixture and using the electric mixer on medium speed, beat until well blended.

Pour the batter into the prepared pan. Sprinkle the hazelnuts evenly over the top and press down gently to lodge the nuts into the batter. Bake until a toothpick inserted into the center of the loaf comes out clean, 50–55 minutes. Let cool in the pan on a wire rack for 10 minutes. Turn the loaf out of the pan onto the rack and let cool completely. Cut into 12 slices to serve.

Pyramid Servings

VEGETABLES	◀○○○○○
FRUITS	◀○○○○○
CARBOHYDRATES	○○○○○○●●
PROTEIN & DAIRY	○○○○○○○
FATS	○○○○●

PER SLICE	
calories	174
kilojoules	728
protein	4 g
carbohydrate	28 g
total fat	6 g
saturated fat	1 g
monounsaturated fat	3 g
cholesterol	35 mg
sodium	79 mg
fiber	2 g

Beans & Legumes

The nutritional value of beans, peas, and lentils is matched only by their versatility in the kitchen.

Black Bean Burgers with Chipotle Ketchup

Spend the time to make the tasty chipotle ketchup, and serve these burgers on whole-grain buns piled with lettuce, tomato, sliced onion, or other extras. Or serve them with a side order of oven-baked fries.

SERVES 6

1¼ cups (9 oz/280 g) dried black beans, picked over and rinsed, soaked overnight, and drained

3 cups (24 fl oz/750 ml) water

2 plum (Roma) tomatoes, peeled and seeded (page 137), then diced

1 yellow onion, chopped

4 cloves garlic, minced

1 tablespoon tomato paste

1 tablespoon wine vinegar

1 chipotle chile, minced

1¾ teaspoons ground cumin

1 teaspoon salt

1½ tablespoons canola oil

½ red bell pepper (capsicum), chopped

½ cup (2½ oz/75 g) cooked brown rice

¼ cup (1 oz/30 g) chopped pecans

1 egg, lightly beaten

¾ cup (1½ oz/45 g) fresh whole-grain bread crumbs

6 whole-grain burger buns

6 slices *each* tomato and red onion

3 lettuce leaves, halved

In a large saucepan over high heat, combine the beans and water. Bring to a boil. Reduce the heat to low, cover partially, and simmer until the beans are tender, 60–70 minutes. Drain.

While the beans are cooking, combine the tomatoes, half of the yellow onion, half of the garlic, the tomato paste, vinegar, chipotle chile, ¾ teaspoon of the cumin, and ¼ teaspoon of the salt in a small saucepan over medium-high heat. Bring the mixture to a boil. Reduce the heat to medium and simmer uncovered, stirring occasionally, until the liquid is reduced and the mixture is a thick sauce, about 5 minutes. Set the chipotle ketchup aside to cool.

In a frying pan, heat ½ tablespoon of the canola oil over medium heat. Add the remaining yellow onion and sauté until soft and translucent, about 4 minutes. Add the bell pepper and remaining garlic and sauté until they soften, about 3 minutes. Stir in ¼ teaspoon of the salt, transfer the mixture to a bowl, and let cool. Set the pan aside.

In a food processor, combine the drained beans, the onion mixture, the brown rice, pecans, the remaining 1 teaspoon cumin, and the remaining ½ teaspoon salt. Pulse several times until the mixture is coarsely puréed. Fold in the beaten egg and bread crumbs. Form the mixture into patties each ¾ inch (2 cm) thick.

In the same pan used for the onion mixture, heat the remaining 1 tablespoon canola oil over medium-high heat. Add the patties and cook, turning once, until nicely browned on both sides and heated through, 7–9 minutes total. Serve each burger on a bun topped with 1 tomato slice, 1 onion slice, ½ lettuce leaf, and a dollop of the ketchup.

Pyramid Servings

VEGETABLES	◀○○○○○
FRUITS	◀○○○○○
CARBOHYDRATES	○○○○○○●●
PROTEIN & DAIRY	○○○○○●●
FATS	○○○○●

PER SERVING	
calories	389
kilojoules	1,628
protein	16 g
carbohydrate	59 g
total fat	11 g
saturated fat	1 g
monounsaturated fat	5 g
cholesterol	35 mg
sodium	791 mg
fiber	15 g

Cannellini Beans with Wilted Greens

Cannellini are a staple in many Italian recipes, such as minestrone. If you can't find them, substitute small white (navy) beans. You can also replace the escarole with spinach, kale, or chard. Serve as a side dish.

SERVES 8

1¼ cups (9 oz/280 g) dried cannellini beans, picked over and rinsed, soaked overnight, and drained

3 cups (24 fl oz/750 ml) water

1 bay leaf

1 tablespoon chopped fresh oregano

4 cloves garlic, 1 left whole and 3 minced

1 tablespoon extra-virgin olive oil

½ yellow onion, chopped

2 tomatoes, seeded and diced

2 anchovy fillets, rinsed and finely chopped (optional)

1 head escarole, about ½ lb (250 g), stemmed and leaves coarsely chopped

½ teaspoon salt

¼ teaspoon freshly ground pepper

2 tablespoons grated Parmesan cheese

In a large saucepan over high heat, combine the beans, water, bay leaf, oregano, and the whole garlic clove. Bring to a boil. Reduce the heat to low, cover partially, and simmer until the beans are tender, 60–75 minutes. Drain and discard the bay leaf and garlic.

In a large saucepan, heat the olive oil over medium-high heat. Add the onion and sauté until lightly golden and soft, about 6 minutes. Add the tomatoes, minced garlic, and the anchovies, if using. Sauté until the tomatoes are softened, about 4 minutes. Stir in the escarole and cooked beans and cook until the greens are wilted and the beans are heated through, about 3 minutes. Season with the salt and pepper and sprinkle with the grated Parmesan. Serve immediately.

Pyramid Servings

VEGETABLES	◀○○○○●
FRUITS	◀○○○○○
CARBOHYDRATES	○○○○○○○○○
PROTEIN & DAIRY	○○○○○○●
FATS	○○○○●

PER SERVING	
calories	143
kilojoules	598
protein	8 g
carbohydrate	23 g
total fat	3 g
saturated fat	1 g
monounsaturated fat	1 g
cholesterol	1 mg
sodium	179 mg
fiber	6 g

Black-Eyed Pea and Sweet Corn Salsa

SERVES 8

A staple in Southern cooking, the black-eyed pea is a cream-colored legume distinguished by a black dot with a white center. This salsa is a perfect partner for grilled fish or chicken. It's also an ideal salad.

Pyramid Servings

VEGETABLES	◀○○○○○
FRUITS	◀○○○○○
CARBOHYDRATES	○○○○○○○○
PROTEIN & DAIRY	○○○○○○●
FATS	○○○○○

PER SERVING	
calories	112
kilojoules	469
protein	6 g
carbohydrate	18 g
total fat	2 g
saturated fat	<1 g
monounsaturated fat	1 g
cholesterol	0 mg
sodium	298 mg
fiber	5 g

In a large saucepan over high heat, combine the peas, water, and ¼ teaspoon of the salt. Bring to a boil. Reduce the heat to low, cover partially, and simmer until the peas are tender, about 45 minutes. Drain the peas, rinse with cool water, drain again, and transfer to a large bowl to cool to room temperature.

In a large nonstick sauté or frying pan, heat the olive oil over medium-high heat. Add the onion and bell pepper and sauté until softened, about 4 minutes. Add the corn, tomato, and garlic and sauté until the tomato is softened and the corn is tender-crisp, about 4 minutes.

Add the corn mixture to the peas along with the lime zest and juice, vinegar, cilantro, the remaining ¼ teaspoon salt, and the pepper. Toss to mix. Serve immediately, or cover and refrigerate for up to 2 days.

1 cup (7 oz/220 g) dried black-eyed peas, picked over and rinsed, soaked overnight, and drained

3 cups (24 fl oz/750 ml) water

½ teaspoon salt

1 tablespoon olive oil

½ yellow onion, chopped

½ green bell pepper (capsicum), seeded and chopped

1 cup (6 oz/185 g) fresh corn kernels (cut from about 2 ears corn)

1 tomato, seeded and diced

1 clove garlic, minced

Grated zest and juice of 1 lime

1 tablespoon white wine vinegar or sherry vinegar

3 tablespoons chopped fresh cilantro (fresh coriander)

¼ teaspoon freshly ground pepper

Three-Bean Chili

SERVES 8

Traditional chili takes on a new look with the addition of colorful roasted bell peppers and kidney, black, and Anasazi beans. Substitute Monterey jack cheese for the *queso asadero* if you like.

Pyramid Servings

VEGETABLES	◀○○○●●
FRUITS	◀○○○○○
CARBOHYDRATES	○○○○○○○○○
PROTEIN & DAIRY	○○○○○●●
FATS	○○○○●

PER SERVING

calories	300
kilojoules	1,255
protein	16 g
carbohydrate	45 g
total fat	8 g
saturated fat	1 g
monounsaturated fat	4 g
cholesterol	5 mg
sodium	486 mg
fiber	16 g

In a large saucepan over high heat, combine the beans, water, bay leaf, and ½ teaspoon of the salt. Bring to a boil. Reduce the heat to low, cover partially, and simmer until the beans are tender but still firm, 60–70 minutes. Drain and discard the bay leaf.

When the beans are cooked, coarsely chop the roasted bell peppers and set aside. In a large saucepan, heat the oil over medium heat. Add the yellow onion and sauté until soft and lightly golden, about 6 minutes. Stir in the garlic, chili powder, oregano, cumin, red pepper flakes, and the remaining 1 teaspoon salt. Cook until fragrant, 1–2 minutes. Add the bell peppers, cooked beans, tomatoes, and cilantro and cook until the tomatoes are heated through, 5–6 minutes.

Ladle the chili into individual bowls and sprinkle with the cheese and green onions.

¾ cup (5 oz/155 g) *each* dried kidney, black, and Anasazi beans, picked over and rinsed, soaked overnight, and drained

4 cups (32 fl oz/1 l) water

1 bay leaf

1½ teaspoons salt

2 large green bell peppers (capsicums), roasted and seeded (page 138)

2 large red bell peppers (capsicums), roasted and seeded (page 138)

3 tablespoons canola oil

1 yellow onion, chopped

4 cloves garlic, minced

1 tablespoon *each* chili powder and dried oregano

2 teaspoons ground cumin

½ teaspoon red pepper flakes

4 tomatoes, peeled and seeded (page 137), then diced

⅓ cup (½ oz/15 g) chopped fresh cilantro (fresh coriander)

6 tablespoons (1½ oz/ 45 g) shredded *queso asadero*

2 green (spring) onions, thinly sliced

Caribbean Red Beans and Brown Rice

Brown rice pairs up with beans in this spicy Caribbean dish. Mix and match brown rice varieties to make your own blend, or purchase a packaged blend. If you can't find small red beans, use kidney beans.

1½ cups (10½ oz/330 g) dried small red beans, picked over and rinsed, soaked overnight, and drained

6½ cups (52 fl oz/1.6 l) water

3 bay leaves

1¼ cups (9 oz/280 g) brown rice

3 tablespoons olive oil

1¼ teaspoons salt

1 yellow onion, chopped

½ green bell pepper (capsicum), seeded and chopped

1 celery stalk, chopped

4 cloves garlic, minced

½ teaspoon *each* ground allspice, cloves, cayenne pepper, and black pepper

1 cup (8 fl oz/250 ml) vegetable stock (page 139) or broth

1 tomato, cored and diced

2 tablespoons chopped fresh thyme

1 teaspoon hot-pepper sauce

3 tablespoons chopped fresh cilantro (fresh coriander)

In a large saucepan over high heat, combine the beans, 4 cups (32 fl oz/1 l) of the water, and the bay leaves. Bring to a boil. Reduce the heat to low, cover partially, and simmer until the beans are tender, 60–70 minutes. Drain and discard the bay leaves.

While the beans are cooking, combine the rice, 1 tablespoon of the oil, ½ teaspoon of the salt, and the remaining 2½ cups (20 fl oz/625 ml) water in a saucepan over medium-high heat. Cover and bring to a boil. Reduce the heat to low and simmer until the water is fully absorbed and the rice is tender, about 45 minutes. Set aside and keep warm.

In a large saucepan, heat the remaining 2 tablespoons oil over medium-high heat. Add the onion, bell pepper, and celery; sauté until the vegetables are softened, 6–8 minutes. Stir in the garlic and cook until softened, about 1 minute. Add the allspice, cloves, cayenne, the remaining ¾ teaspoon salt, and the black pepper. Cook for 1 minute. Stir in the cooked beans, the vegetable stock, tomato, thyme, and hot-pepper sauce. Cook until the vegetable mixture is heated through, 6–8 minutes.

Divide the rice among warmed individual bowls. Top each serving with beans and sprinkle with the cilantro.

Pyramid Servings

VEGETABLES	◀ ○○○○●
FRUITS	◀ ○○○○○
CARBOHYDRATES	○○○○○○●●
PROTEIN & DAIRY	○○○○○●●
FATS	○○○○●

PER SERVING	
calories	382
kilojoules	1,598
protein	14 g
carbohydrate	63 g
total fat	9 g
saturated fat	1 g
monounsaturated fat	5 g
cholesterol	0 mg
sodium	517 mg
fiber	11 g

Sesame-Crusted Tofu

Serve these "steaks" with soy sauce and a green-onion garnish. Be sure to use firm tofu. Brown it gently so it loses some moisture before coating it with bread crumbs and sesame seeds, then browning again.

SERVES 4

1 lb (500 g) firm tofu, drained

¼ cup (2 fl oz/60 ml) nonfat milk

2 egg whites, lightly beaten

½ teaspoon salt

¼ teaspoon freshly ground pepper

3 tablespoons plain dried bread crumbs

2 tablespoons white sesame seeds

1 tablespoon black sesame seeds

½ teaspoon sesame oil or canola oil

12 green (spring) onions, ends trimmed, cut in half crosswise, then halved again lengthwise

Cut the tofu crosswise into 12 slices. Place the tofu slices in a large nonstick frying pan over medium heat and cook for 5 minutes on each side. The tofu will brown slightly and lose some of its liquid. Transfer to a plate and let cool.

In a bowl, whisk together the milk, egg whites, ¼ teaspoon of the salt, and the pepper until well blended. On a large plate, combine the bread crumbs, white and black sesame seeds, and the remaining ¼ teaspoon salt. Mix until well blended. Dip a tofu slice into the milk mixture, then dredge in the sesame seed mixture. Repeat dipping and dredging with the remaining tofu slices.

In a large nonstick frying pan, heat the oil over medium heat. Arrange the coated tofu slices in the pan and cook, turning once, until lightly browned, about 3 minutes on each side. Transfer to a plate and keep warm. Add the green onions to the pan and sauté until they begin to brown, 3–4 minutes.

Divide the green onions among individual plates. Top each serving with 3 tofu steaks and serve immediately.

Pyramid Servings

VEGETABLES	◄●○○○○
FRUITS	◄○○○○○
CARBOHYDRATES	○○○○○○○○
PROTEIN & DAIRY	○○○○○●●
FATS	○○○○●

PER SERVING	
calories	265
kilojoules	1,109
protein	24 g
carbohydrate	17 g
total fat	14 g
saturated fat	2 g
monounsaturated fat	4 g
cholesterol	0 mg
sodium	391 mg
fiber	6 g

Classic Boston Baked Beans

The rich flavor of this hearty side dish comes from slow-roasted navy beans, onion, molasses, dry mustard, and a bit of smoky bacon. For a vegetarian version, replace the bacon with four drops of liquid smoke.

SERVES 12

2 cups (14 oz/440 g) dried small white (navy) beans, picked over and rinsed, soaked overnight, and drained

4 cups (32 fl oz/1 l) water

2 bay leaves

¾ teaspoon salt

1 yellow onion, chopped

½ cup (5½ oz/170 g) light molasses

1½ tablespoons dry mustard

3 strips thick-cut bacon, cut into ½-inch (12-mm) pieces

In a large, ovenproof pot with a tight-fitting lid or a Dutch oven, combine the beans, water, bay leaves, and ½ teaspoon of the salt over high heat. Bring to a boil. Reduce the heat to low, cover partially, and simmer until the beans have softened but are still firm, 65–75 minutes. Remove from the heat and discard the bay leaves. Do not drain the beans.

Preheat the oven to 350°F (180°C).

Stir the onion, molasses, mustard, bacon, and the remaining ¼ teaspoon salt into the beans. Cover and bake until the beans are tender and coated with a light syrup, 4½–5 hours. Check periodically to make sure the beans don't dry out, stirring and adding hot water as needed.

Pyramid Servings

VEGETABLES	◀○○○○○
FRUITS	◀○○○○○
CARBOHYDRATES	○○○○○○○○
PROTEIN & DAIRY	○○○○○●●
FATS	○○○○○

PER SERVING	
calories	200
kilojoules	837
protein	9 g
carbohydrate	33 g
total fat	4 g
saturated fat	1 g
monounsaturated fat	2 g
cholesterol	4 mg
sodium	197 mg
fiber	6 g

Fish & Shellfish

Seafoods, whether caught in the wild or farm-reared, are among the wisest main-course choices a cook can make.

Mahimahi
with Macadamia Nut Crust

Baking these nut-crusted fillets in the upper third of the oven lets them brown nicely without the addition of oil. Serve with a side of Green Beans with Red Pepper and Garlic (page 31).

SERVES 4

¼ cup (½ oz/15 g) fresh whole-grain bread crumbs

3 tablespoons macadamia nuts, finely chopped

1 tablespoon finely chopped fresh flat-leaf (Italian) parsley

½ teaspoon grated lemon zest

½ teaspoon salt

¼ cup (2 fl oz/60 ml) nonfat milk

4 mahimahi fillets, each 5 oz (155 g) and about 1 inch (2.5 cm) thick

¼ teaspoon freshly ground pepper

Place a rack in the upper third of the oven and preheat to 450°F (230°C). Place a small wire rack in a shallow non-stick baking pan.

On a plate, stir together the bread crumbs, nuts, parsley, lemon zest, and ¼ teaspoon of the salt. Pour the milk into a shallow dish. Dip each fillet in the milk and then dredge in the nut mixture, coating completely and pressing down lightly so the mixture adheres well.

Place the fillets on the rack in the baking pan, making sure that they do not touch. Sprinkle evenly with the remaining ¼ teaspoon salt and the pepper.

Bake until the fish is opaque throughout when tested with the tip of a knife and the crust is golden brown, 10–12 minutes. Transfer to warmed individual plates and serve immediately.

Pyramid Servings

VEGETABLES	◄○○○○○
FRUITS	◄○○○○○
CARBOHYDRATES	○○○○○○○●
PROTEIN & DAIRY	○○○○○○○●
FATS	○○○○○

PER SERVING	
calories	180
kilojoules	753
protein	28 g
carbohydrate	3 g
total fat	6 g
saturated fat	1 g
monounsaturated fat	4 g
cholesterol	104 mg
sodium	462 mg
fiber	1 g

Pan-Braised Swordfish with Feta

SERVES 4

This Mediterranean-style swordfish dish goes from stove to table in less than 20 minutes. Serve it alongside steamed zucchini or Asparagus with Hazelnut Gremolata (page 34).

Pyramid Servings

VEGETABLES	◀○○○○○
FRUITS	◀○○○○●
CARBOHYDRATES	○○○○○○○○○
PROTEIN & DAIRY	○○○○○●●
FATS	○○○○○

PER SERVING	
calories	277
kilojoules	1,159
protein	30 g
carbohydrate	19 g
total fat	9 g
saturated fat	3 g
monounsaturated fat	4 g
cholesterol	59 mg
sodium	700 mg
fiber	1 g

Sprinkle the swordfish steaks on both sides with ¼ teaspoon of the salt and ⅛ teaspoon of the pepper. In a large, nonstick frying pan, heat 1 teaspoon of the oil over medium-high heat. Add the fish to the pan and sear on both sides until lightly browned, about 2 minutes on each side. Transfer to a plate and keep warm.

Reduce the heat to medium and add the remaining ½ teaspoon oil to the pan. Add the onion and garlic and sauté for 1 minute. Stir in the stock, raisins, and vinegar. Return the swordfish to the pan and top with the lemon slices. Cover and simmer until the fish is opaque throughout when tested with the tip of a knife, 3–4 minutes.

Remove the lemon slices from the fish and set aside. Transfer the swordfish steaks to warmed individual plates. Stir the feta, the remaining ½ teaspoon salt and ⅛ teaspoon pepper, the marjoram, and the capers into the pan juices. Remove from the heat. Spoon some sauce over each swordfish steak and top with the reserved lemon slices. Serve immediately.

4 swordfish steaks,
  each 5 oz (155 g) and
  ¾–1 inch (2–2.5 cm) thick

¾ teaspoon salt

¼ teaspoon freshly ground
  pepper

1½ teaspoons olive oil or
  canola oil

1 red onion, thinly sliced

2 cloves garlic, minced

1 cup (8 fl oz/250 ml)
  vegetable stock
  (page 139) or broth

½ cup (3 oz/90 g) golden
  raisins (sultanas)

2 tablespoons red wine
  vinegar

1 small lemon, thinly sliced

2 tablespoons crumbled
  feta cheese

1 tablespoon chopped
  fresh marjoram or
  oregano

1 tablespoon capers,
  rinsed

Seared Salmon with Cilantro-Cucumber Salsa

SERVES 4

Here, a summertime salsa contributes color, flavor, and texture to basic pan-seared salmon. You can make the salsa several hours in advance and refrigerate it until you are ready to serve.

Pyramid Servings

VEGETABLES	◀ ○○○○●
FRUITS	◀ ○○○○○
CARBOHYDRATES	○○○○○○○○○
PROTEIN & DAIRY	○○○○○●●
FATS	○○○○●

PER SERVING	
calories	243
kilojoules	1,017
protein	29 g
carbohydrate	6 g
total fat	11 g
saturated fat	2 g
monounsaturated fat	4 g
cholesterol	78 mg
sodium	654 mg
fiber	1 g

In a bowl, combine the cucumber, tomatoes, bell pepper, shallot, and chopped cilantro. Toss gently to mix. In a small bowl, whisk together the lime juice, 1 teaspoon of the canola oil, the honey, red pepper flakes, and ½ teaspoon of the salt. Pour the lime juice mixture over the cucumber mixture and toss gently to mix and coat evenly. Set aside.

Sprinkle the salmon fillets on both sides with the remaining ½ teaspoon salt and the black pepper. In a large, non-stick frying pan, heat the remaining ½ teaspoon canola oil over medium-high heat. Add the fish to the pan and cook, turning once, until opaque throughout when tested with the tip of a knife, 4–5 minutes on each side.

Transfer the salmon fillets to warmed individual plates and top each with one-fourth of the salsa. Garnish the plates with the cilantro sprigs and lime wedges. Serve immediately.

½ cucumber, peeled, halved lengthwise, seeded, halved length-wise again, and thinly sliced crosswise

1 cup (6 oz/185 g) cherry tomatoes, quartered

½ yellow or orange bell pepper (capsicum), seeded and cut into 1-inch (2.5-cm) julienne

2 tablespoons chopped shallot or red onion

1 tablespoon chopped fresh cilantro (fresh coriander), plus sprigs for garnish

1 tablespoon fresh lime juice

1½ teaspoons canola oil

1 teaspoon honey

½ teaspoon red pepper flakes

1 teaspoon salt

4 salmon fillets, each 5 oz (155 g) and about 1 inch (2.5 cm) thick

¼ teaspoon freshly ground black pepper

Lime wedges for garnish

Prawns Puttanesca

SERVES 4

Rich with Mediterranean flavors—olives, anchovies, capers—this sauce cooks in 5 minutes, retaining its freshness when tossed with shrimp. Accompany with sautéed kale or steamed broccoli and pasta.

Pyramid Servings

VEGETABLES	◀○○●●●
FRUITS	◀○○○○○
CARBOHYDRATES	○○○○○○○○○
PROTEIN & DAIRY	○○○○○○●
FATS	○○○○○

PER SERVING	
calories	284
kilojoules	1,188
protein	31 g
carbohydrate	23 g
total fat	8 g
saturated fat	1 g
monounsaturated fat	4 g
cholesterol	132 mg
sodium	588 mg
fiber	4 g

In a large, nonstick sauté or frying pan, heat the olive oil over medium-high heat. Add the shrimp, sprinkle with the salt and black pepper, and cook for about 3 minutes. Turn the shrimp and cook until opaque and pink, about 2 minutes longer. Transfer to a bowl and keep warm.

Add the wine and deglaze pan, stirring with a wooden spoon to scrape up any browned bits. Add the fresh and sun-dried tomatoes and the garlic. Reduce the heat to medium and simmer until the tomatoes are tender, about 3 minutes.

Add all the remaining ingredients and cook for about 2 minutes longer to allow the flavors to blend. Return the shrimp to the pan and toss well to coat. Serve immediately.

1 tablespoon olive oil

1¼ lb (625 g) large shrimp (prawns), peeled and deveined

½ teaspoon salt

½ teaspoon freshly ground black pepper

2 tablespoons dry white wine

4 tomatoes, peeled and seeded (page 137), then diced

¼ cup (2 oz/60 g) dry-packed sun-dried tomatoes, soaked in water to rehydrate, drained, and chopped

3 cloves garlic, minced

¼ cup (1½ oz/45 g) chopped pitted Niçoise olives

2 tablespoons capers, rinsed and chopped

6 anchovy fillets, rinsed and finely chopped

1 tablespoon grated lemon zest

1 tablespoon chopped fresh parsley

1 tablespoon chopped fresh basil

½ teaspoon red pepper flakes (optional)

Roasted Red Snapper

Dinner guests will be impressed with both the bright flavors and the look of this roasted whole fish. Yet it couldn't be simpler to prepare. Serve it with a salad and with crusty bread for soaking up the juices.

½ cup (4 fl oz/125 ml) fresh orange juice

½ cup (4 fl oz/125 ml) fresh lime juice

½ teaspoon grated orange zest

½ teaspoon grated lime zest

3 shallots or ½ red onion, chopped

2 tablespoons olive oil

1 small whole red snapper, about 1½ lb (750 g), cleaned and scaled, head and tail left on

2 cloves garlic, coarsely chopped

2 tablespoons chopped fresh basil

2 tablespoons chopped fresh mint

1 tablespoon chopped fresh thyme

1 teaspoon salt

½ teaspoon coarsely ground pepper

1 small leek, including tender green top, halved lengthwise, and cut crosswise into 1½-inch (4-cm) pieces

2 large tomatoes, cut crosswise into slices ½ inch (12 mm) thick

In a shallow glass baking dish, combine the orange and lime juices and zests, shallots, and 1 tablespoon of the oil.

Score the skin of the fish in a diamond pattern. Add the fish to the marinade and turn once to coat. Cover and refrigerate for 30 minutes, turning the fish occasionally.

Preheat the oven to 425°F (220°C). Lightly coat a shallow baking dish with cooking spray.

In a blender or small food processor, combine the garlic, basil, mint, thyme, the remaining 1 tablespoon oil, ½ teaspoon of the salt, and ¼ teaspoon of the pepper. Pulse to purée. In a small bowl, combine half of the herb paste with the leek. Toss gently to mix.

Sprinkle the leek mixture evenly over the bottom of the prepared baking dish. Top with the tomato slices, arranging them in a single layer. Sprinkle the tomatoes with the remaining ½ teaspoon salt and ¼ teaspoon pepper. Remove the fish from the marinade and pat dry. Discard the marinade. Rub the remaining herb paste over the fish, coating both sides. Place the fish on top of the tomatoes and cover the dish tightly with aluminum foil.

Roast the fish for 30 minutes, then uncover and roast until the fish is opaque throughout when tested with the tip of a knife, 10–12 minutes longer. Lift the fish from the baking dish and place on a large platter. Divide the vegetables among 4 warmed individual plates. Peel the skin from the top of the fish, remove the top fillet, and divide it between 2 of the plates. Lift out the center fish bone and discard. Lift the second fillet and divide it between the remaining 2 plates. Serve immediately.

Pyramid Servings

VEGETABLES	◀○○○●●
FRUITS	◀○○○○○
CARBOHYDRATES	○○○○○○○○○
PROTEIN & DAIRY	○○○○○●●
FATS	○○○○○

PER SERVING	
calories	285
kilojoules	1,192
protein	37 g
carbohydrate	14 g
total fat	8 g
saturated fat	1 g
monounsaturated fat	5 g
cholesterol	63 mg
sodium	712 mg
fiber	2 g

Poultry & Meat

Poultry and meats can often step back from the center of the plate, taking on a supporting role.

Chicken Stir-Fry with Eggplant and Basil, page 122

Turkey Potpie
with Baby Vegetables

This old-fashioned potpie has just a top crust, made with cornmeal and a hint of honey. The easy filling can be made a day ahead. Then mix the batter while the oven heats, and the pie is ready to assemble.

SERVES **8**

10 baby carrots

1 cup (7 oz/220 g) pearl onions

⅓ lb (155 g) fresh white mushrooms

1¼ cups (8 oz/250 g) frozen artichoke hearts

¼ cup (2 fl oz/60 ml) plus 2 tablespoons olive oil

1 teaspoon dry mustard

¾ cup (4 oz/120 g) all-purpose (plain) flour

2½ cups (20 fl oz/625 ml) chicken stock or broth

1 clove garlic, minced

2 lb (1 kg) skinless, bone-less turkey breast, diced

1 cup (5 oz/155 g) shelled edamame or English peas

1 tomato, seeded and diced

1 tablespoon *each* fresh chopped dill and basil

¼ cup (2 oz/60 g) low-fat sour cream

1½ teaspoons salt

½ cup (2½ oz/75 g) cornmeal

1½ teaspoons baking powder

¾ cup (6 fl oz/180 ml) plain soy milk (soya milk)

1 tablespoon dark honey

Peel and halve the carrots, then thinly slice crosswise. Immerse the onions in a saucepan of boiling water for about 2 minutes, drain, and plunge in cold water. Cut off the root ends, slip off the skins, and then cut a shallow X in the root end of each onion. Brush the mushrooms clean, then thinly slice. Let the artichokes thaw fully, then quarter them lengthwise. Set the prepared vegetables aside.

In a large, heavy, ovenproof saucepan or Dutch oven, heat the ¼ cup olive oil over low heat. Add the mustard and ¼ cup (1½ oz/45 g) of the flour and cook, whisking constantly, for 1–2 minutes.

Add the stock, still whisking constantly to avoid lumps, raise the heat to medium-high, and bring to a boil. Add the garlic, carrots, and onions. Reduce the heat to a low simmer and cook until the vegetables are softened, about 5 minutes. Add the turkey, mushrooms, artichoke hearts, edamame, tomato, dill, and basil. Cover and simmer until the turkey is opaque throughout, about 10 minutes. Whisk in the sour cream and season with 1 teaspoon of the salt. Spoon the turkey mixture into a 9-by-13-inch (23-by-33-cm) baking dish and set aside.

Preheat the oven to 425°F (220°C). In a bowl, combine the cornmeal, the remaining ½ cup (2½ oz/75 g) flour, baking powder, and the remaining ½ teaspoon salt. In another bowl, whisk together the soy milk, the 2 table-spoons olive oil, and the honey. Add the dry ingredients, stirring just until moistened.

Pour the batter over the turkey mixture. Bake, uncovered, until lightly browned, about 40 minutes. Let stand for 10 minutes, then serve.

Pyramid Servings

VEGETABLES	◄○○○●●
FRUITS	◄○○○○○
CARBOHYDRATES	○○○○○○○●
PROTEIN & DAIRY	○○○○○●●
FATS	○○○○●

PER SERVING	
calories	384
kilojoules	1,607
protein	30 g
carbohydrate	34 g
total fat	14 g
saturated fat	3 g
monounsaturated fat	8 g
cholesterol	51 mg
sodium	657 mg
fiber	5 g

Roasted Rack of Lamb with Parsley Crust

SERVES 4

For special occasions, a rack of lamb is an elegant main course that is simple to prepare. Serve it with Asparagus with Hazelnut Gremolata (page 34) and Two-Potato Gratin (page 43).

Pyramid Servings

VEGETABLES	◀○○○○○
FRUITS	◀○○○○○
CARBOHYDRATES	○○○○○○○○○
PROTEIN & DAIRY	○○○○○●●
FATS	○○○○○

PER SERVING	
calories	207
kilojoules	867
protein	28 g
carbohydrate	5 g
total fat	8 g
saturated fat	3 g
monounsaturated fat	3 g
cholesterol	86 mg
sodium	514 mg
fiber	1 g

Preheat the oven to 450°F (230°C).

Place the bread in a blender or food processor and pulse until it forms coarse crumbs. Add the parsley, thyme, and garlic; pulse to blend.

Season the racks of lamb with the salt and pepper. In a heavy ovenproof frying pan, heat the olive oil over medium-high heat. Add the lamb to the pan and cook, turning as needed, until browned on all sides, about 5 minutes. Remove the pan from the heat and brush the mustard over the rounded top and front of the racks (but not the underside of the bones.) Gently pat the bread crumb mixture into the mustard.

Roast until an instant-read thermometer inserted into the meat (but not touching the bone) reads 140°F (60°C) for medium-rare, 20–25 minutes. Transfer to a platter and let rest for 10 minutes.

To serve, cut the lamb between the ribs into separate bone-in chops and place on warmed individual plates.

1 slice (½ oz/15 g) whole-wheat (wholemeal) bread

2 tablespoons chopped fresh flat-leaf (Italian) parsley

1 tablespoon chopped fresh thyme

2 cloves garlic, minced

2 racks of lamb, frenched, about 1 lb (500 g) each, trimmed of visible fat

½ teaspoon salt

¼ teaspoon freshly ground pepper

½ teaspoon olive oil

1 tablespoon Dijon mustard

Chicken Stir-Fry with Eggplant and Basil

SERVES 4

This colorful main dish requires a fair amount of chopping, slicing, and dicing, but the cooking takes only minutes. Serve with stir-fried broccoli and cauliflower and brown basmati rice.

Pyramid Servings

VEGETABLES	◀○○●●●
FRUITS	◀○○○○○
CARBOHYDRATES	○○○○○○○○
PROTEIN & DAIRY	○○○○○○●
FATS	○○○○●

PER SERVING	
calories	248
kilojoules	1,167
protein	30 g
carbohydrate	13 g
total fat	8 g
saturated fat	1 g
monounsaturated fat	5 g
cholesterol	66 mg
sodium	408 mg
fiber	4 g

In a blender or food processor, combine the basil, mint, ¼ cup (2 fl oz/60 m) of the stock, the chopped green onions, garlic, and ginger. Pulse until the mixture is minced but not puréed. Set aside.

In a large, nonstick frying pan, heat 1 tablespoon of the olive oil over medium-high heat. Add the eggplant, yellow onion, and bell peppers and sauté until the vegetables are just tender, about 8 minutes. Transfer to a bowl and cover with a kitchen towel to keep warm.

Add the remaining 1 tablespoon olive oil to the pan and heat over medium-high heat. Add the basil mixture and sauté for about 1 minute, stirring constantly. Add the chicken strips and soy sauce and sauté until the chicken is almost opaque throughout, about 2 minutes. Add the remaining ½ cup (4 fl oz/120 ml) stock and bring to a boil. Return the eggplant mixture to the pan and stir until heated through, about 3 minutes. Transfer to a warmed serving dish and garnish with the sliced green onion. Serve immediately.

¼ cup (⅓ oz/10 g) coarsely chopped fresh basil

2 tablespoons chopped fresh mint

¾ cup (6 fl oz/180 ml) chicken stock or broth

3 green (spring) onions, including tender green tops, 2 coarsely chopped and 1 thinly sliced

2 cloves garlic

1 tablespoon peeled and chopped fresh ginger

2 tablespoons extra-virgin olive oil

1 small eggplant (aubergine), with peel, diced (about 4 cups/ 13 oz/410 g)

1 yellow onion, coarsely chopped

1 red bell pepper (capsicum), seeded and cut into julienne

1 yellow bell pepper (capsicum), seeded and cut into julienne

1 lb (500 g) skinless, boneless chicken breasts, cut into strips ½ inch (12 mm) wide and 2 inches (5 cm) long

2 tablespoons low-sodium soy sauce

Beef Stew
with Fennel and Shallots

The rich flavor of this stew gets a boost from portobello mushrooms and fresh fennel. For a hearty supper, serve it with Double-Corn Spoon Bread (page 82). And keep in mind, the wine is optional.

SERVES 6

3 tablespoons all-purpose (plain) flour

1 lb (500 g) boneless lean beef stew meat, trimmed of visible fat and cut into 1½-inch (4-cm) cubes

2 tablespoons olive oil

½ fennel bulb, trimmed and thinly sliced vertically (about 1 cup/3 oz/90 g)

3 large shallots, chopped

1½ teaspoons salt

¾ teaspoon pepper

2 fresh thyme sprigs

1 bay leaf

3 cups (24 fl oz/750 ml) vegetable stock or broth

½ cup (4 fl oz/125 ml) red wine (optional)

4 large carrots, peeled and cut into 1-inch (2.5-cm) chunks

4 large red-skinned potatoes, peeled and cut into 1-inch (2.5-cm) chunks

18 small boiling onions, about 10 oz (315 g) total weight, halved crosswise

3 portobello mushrooms, cut into 1-inch (2.5-cm) chunks

⅓ cup (½ oz/15 g) finely chopped fresh parsley

Place the flour on a plate. Dredge the beef cubes in the flour. In a large, heavy saucepan, heat the oil over medium heat. Add the beef and cook, turning as needed, until browned on all sides, about 5 minutes. Remove the beef from the pan with a slotted spoon and set aside.

Add the fennel and shallots to the pan over medium heat and sauté until softened and lightly golden, 7–8 minutes. Add ½ teaspoon of the salt, ¼ teaspoon of the pepper, the thyme sprigs, and the bay leaf and sauté for 1 minute. Return the beef to the pan and add the vegetable stock and the wine, if using. Bring to a boil, then reduce the heat to low, cover, and simmer gently until the meat is tender, 40–45 minutes.

Add the carrots, potatoes, onions, and mushrooms. (The liquid will not cover the vegetables completely, but more liquid will accumulate as the mushrooms soften.) Simmer gently until the vegetables are tender, about 30 minutes longer. Discard the thyme sprigs and bay leaf. Stir in the parsley and the remaining 1 teaspoon salt and remaining ½ teaspoon pepper.

Ladle the stew into warmed individual bowls and serve immediately.

Pyramid Servings

VEGETABLES	◀○○●●●
FRUITS	◀○○○○○
CARBOHYDRATES	○○○○○○○●
PROTEIN & DAIRY	○○○○○○○●
FATS	○○○○○

PER SERVING	
calories	318
kilojoules	1,331
protein	21 g
carbohydrate	36 g
total fat	11 g
saturated fat	3 g
monounsaturated fat	6 g
cholesterol	47 mg
sodium	677 mg
fiber	6 g

Desserts

The very best sweets can be creamy, crunchy, juicy, and even rich tasting and still be good for you.

Summer Fruit Gratin

SERVES 6

Although this dessert uses a mix of summer stone fruits, it can be easily adapted. In early summer, combine raspberries and apricots; in the fall, try a combination of apples and cranberries.

Pyramid Servings

VEGETABLES	◀○○○○○
FRUITS	◀○○○●●
CARBOHYDRATES	○○○○○○○●
PROTEIN & DAIRY	○○○○○○○
FATS	○○○○●

PER SERVING	
calories	224
kilojoules	937
protein	4 g
carbohydrate	38 g
total fat	8 g
saturated fat	1 g
monounsaturated fat	3 g
cholesterol	0 mg
sodium	52 mg
fiber	5 g

Preheat the oven to 350°F (180°C). Lightly coat a 9-inch (23-cm) square baking dish with cooking spray.

In a bowl, combine the cherries and stone fruits. Sprinkle with the flour and turbinado sugar and toss gently to mix.

To make the topping, in another bowl, combine the oats, almonds, flour, turbinado sugar, cinnamon, nutmeg, and salt. Whisk to blend. Stir in the oil and honey and mix until well blended.

Spread the fruit mixture evenly in the prepared baking dish. Sprinkle the oat-almond mixture evenly over the fruit. Bake until the fruit is bubbling and the topping is lightly browned, 45–55 minutes. Serve warm or at room temperature.

1 lb (500 g) cherries, pitted and halved

4 cups (1½ lb/750 g) peeled, pitted, and sliced mixed summer stone fruits such as nectarines, peaches, and apricots

1 tablespoon whole-wheat (wholemeal) flour

1 tablespoon turbinado sugar or firmly packed light brown sugar

FOR THE TOPPING

½ cup (1½ oz/45 g) old-fashioned rolled oats

¼ cup (1 oz/30 g) sliced (flaked) almonds

3 tablespoons whole-wheat (wholemeal) flour

2 tablespoons turbinado sugar or firmly packed light brown sugar

¼ teaspoon ground cinnamon

⅛ teaspoon ground nutmeg

⅛ teaspoon salt

2 tablespoons walnut oil or canola oil

1 tablespoon dark honey

Caramelized Pear Bread Pudding

SERVES 8

Raisins are often the fruit of choice in bread puddings, but in this classy version caramelized fresh pears are used both in and on top of the pudding. Serve it for dessert or feature it at breakfast or brunch.

Pyramid Servings

VEGETABLES	◀○○○○○
FRUITS	◀○○○○●
CARBOHYDRATES	○○○○○○○●
PROTEIN & DAIRY	○○○○○○●
FATS	○○○○●

PER SERVING	
calories	255
kilojoules	1,067
protein	7 g
carbohydrate	43 g
total fat	8 g
saturated fat	2 g
monounsaturated fat	3 g
cholesterol	60 mg
sodium	175 mg
fiber	8 g

Preheat the oven to 350°F (180°C). Lightly coat a 9-inch (23-cm) square baking dish with cooking spray.

Arrange the bread cubes in a single layer on a baking sheet. Bake until lightly toasted, about 5 minutes. Set the toasted cubes aside.

In a large, nonstick frying pan, melt 1½ teaspoons of the butter over medium heat until frothy. Stir in 1 tablespoon of the canola oil. Add half of the pear slices to the pan and sauté until evenly browned, about 10 minutes. Sprinkle a generous pinch of allspice onto the pears, then transfer them to a plate. Repeat with the remaining butter, oil, pears, and allspice.

Arrange half of the toasted bread cubes evenly in the bottom of the prepared baking dish. Top with half of the sautéed pears and then the remaining bread cubes.

In a large bowl, combine the milk, eggs, 2 tablespoons of the turbinado sugar, the honey, vanilla, cinnamon, and cloves. Whisk until well blended. Pour the milk mixture over the bread and cover with plastic wrap. Let stand for 20–30 minutes, pressing down gently every so often until the bread absorbs the milk mixture. Remove the plastic wrap and arrange the remaining pears on top. Sprinkle with the remaining 1 tablespoon turbinado sugar.

Bake until a knife inserted into the center of the pudding comes out clean, 45–55 minutes. Let cool for 10 minutes before serving.

12 oz (375 g) sturdy multigrain bread, cut into 1-inch (2.5-cm) cubes

1 tablespoon unsalted butter

2 tablespoons canola oil

3 large, firm yet ripe pears, peeled, halved, cored, and thinly sliced

2 pinches of allspice

2¾ cups (22 fl oz/680 ml) 1-percent low-fat milk

2 eggs, lightly beaten

3 tablespoons turbinado sugar or firmly packed light brown sugar

2 tablespoons dark honey

2 teaspoons vanilla extract (essence)

1 teaspoon ground cinnamon

⅛ teaspoon ground cloves

Almond and Apricot Biscotti

These classic twice-baked cookies get some extra flavor and crunch from whole-wheat flour. For variety, try making them with pecans or walnuts and raisins, dried cherries, or dried blueberries.

MAKES **24** COOKIES

¾ cup (4 oz/125 g) whole-wheat (wholemeal) flour

¾ cup (4 oz/125 g) all-purpose (plain) flour

¼ cup (2 oz/60 g) firmly packed brown sugar

1 teaspoon baking powder

2 eggs, lightly beaten

¼ cup (2 fl oz/60 ml) 1-percent low-fat milk

2½ tablespoons canola oil

2 tablespoons dark honey

½ teaspoon almond extract (essence)

⅔ cup (4 oz/125 g) chopped dried apricots

¼ cup (1 oz/30 g) coarsely chopped almonds

Preheat the oven to 350°F (180°C).

In a large bowl, combine the flours, brown sugar, and baking powder. Whisk to blend. Add the eggs, milk, canola oil, honey, and almond extract. Stir with a wooden spoon until the dough just begins to come together. Add the chopped apricots and almonds. With floured hands, mix until the dough is well blended.

Place the dough on a long sheet of plastic wrap and shape by hand into a flattened log 12 inches (30 cm) long, 3 inches (7.5 cm) wide, and about 1 inch (2.5 cm) high. Lift the plastic wrap to invert the dough onto a nonstick baking sheet. Bake until lightly browned, 25–30 minutes. Transfer to another baking sheet to cool for 10 minutes. Leave the oven set at 350°F.

Place the cooled log on a cutting board. With a serrated knife, cut crosswise on the diagonal into 24 slices ½ inch (12 mm) wide. Arrange the slices, cut side down, on the baking sheet. Return to the oven and bake until crisp, 15–20 minutes. Transfer to a wire rack and let cool completely. Store in an airtight container.

Pyramid Servings

VEGETABLES	◀○○○○○
FRUITS	◀○○○○○
CARBOHYDRATES	○○○○○○○●
PROTEIN & DAIRY	○○○○○○○
FATS	○○○○○

PER **3** COOKIES	
calories	79
kilojoules	331
protein	2 g
carbohydrate	12 g
total fat	3 g
saturated fat	0 g
monounsaturated fat	1 g
cholesterol	18 mg
sodium	37 mg
fiber	1 g

Date-Walnut Cake
with Warm Honey Sauce

SERVES 8

This easy single-layer cake is moist and sweet. To make a sheet cake or two-layer cake for a special occasion, double the recipe. You can also substitute fresh Medjool dates for the dried dates.

Pyramid Servings

VEGETABLES ◀○○○○○
FRUITS ◀○○○●●
CARBOHYDRATES ○○○○○○●●
PROTEIN & DAIRY ○○○○○○○
FATS ○○○○●

PER SERVING	
calories	300
kilojoules	1,255
protein	6 g
carbohydrate	48 g
total fat	10 g
saturated fat	1 g
monounsaturated fat	5 g
cholesterol	54 mg
sodium	154 mg
fiber	2 g

Preheat the oven to 350°F (180°C). Lightly coat a 9-inch (23-cm) round cake pan with cooking spray.

In a large bowl, combine the oats and boiling water. Stir to mix. Let stand until the water is absorbed, about 20 minutes. Stir in the brown sugar, ¼ cup of the honey, and the canola oil. Add the eggs, one at a time, beating well after each addition. Stir in the vanilla.

In a small bowl, combine the flours, cinnamon, baking soda, ¼ teaspoon of the nutmeg, and the salt. Whisk to blend. Add the flour mixture to the oat mixture, alternating with the buttermilk, beginning and ending with the flour mixture. Gently fold in the dates and walnuts.

Pour the batter into the prepared pan and bake until the cake springs back when touched lightly in the center, 25–30 minutes. Place the pan on a wire rack to cool slightly. Transfer the cake to a serving plate.

In a small, heavy saucepan over medium-low heat, combine the milk and the remaining ¼ teaspoon nutmeg and bring to a simmer. Whisk in the remaining ¼ cup honey, raise the heat to medium, and bring to a boil, stirring constantly. Continue cooking and stirring until the mixture thickens slightly, about 3 minutes.

Cut the cake into 8 wedges and serve warm or at room temperature. Drizzle with the warm honey sauce.

¾ cup (2½ oz/75 g) old-fashioned rolled oats

1 cup (8 fl oz/250 ml) boiling water

¼ cup (2 oz/60 g) firmly packed light brown sugar

½ cup (6 oz/180 g) dark honey

¼ cup (2 fl oz/60 ml) canola oil

2 eggs

1 teaspoon vanilla extract (essence)

¾ cup (4 oz/125 g) all-purpose (plain) flour

½ cup (2 oz/60 g) whole-wheat (wholemeal) cake (soft-wheat) flour

1 teaspoon ground cinnamon

½ teaspoon baking soda (bicarbonate of soda)

½ teaspoon ground nutmeg

⅛ teaspoon salt

⅓ cup (30 fl oz/80 ml) low-fat buttermilk

¼ cup (3 oz/90 g) chopped dried dates

1½ tablespoons chopped walnuts

½ cup (4 fl oz/125 ml) 1-percent low-fat milk

GLOSSARY

The ingredients used in this cookbook, many of which are described in this glossary, can be found in most well-stocked supermarkets or natural-foods stores. However, several items, such as chipotle chiles, are easiest to find in specialty markets. Farmers' markets are a great source of uncommon fresh fruits and vegetables.

ANCHOVIES These tiny fillets of sardinelike fish, preserved in salt and most often sold packed in oil, can add richness to a range of dishes from pastas to vinaigrettes. When used in small quantities, they have little impact on fat or sodium levels. Anchovy paste, sold in squeeze tubes, can be substituted in recipes in which the anchovies are minced, crushed, or blended.

AVOCADOS Hass avocados have a pebbly skin that ripens from green to purple-black and firm, buttery flesh. Fuertes avocados remain green and have a lighter flavor. Choose hard avocados and let them ripen at room temperature. A ripe avocado dents easily when pressed at the stem end. Although avocados are high in fat, it's mostly the monounsaturated kind that helps lower cholesterol. They also contain beta-sitosterol, glutathione, and vitamin E, all of which have health benefits.

BALSAMIC VINEGAR At its best, balsamic vinegar is a costly condiment, made from wine grapes and aged in barrels, to be enjoyed drop by drop on vegetables, fruits, or ice cream. At its worst, it is an overly sweet, caramel-colored vinegar that can overwhelm a dish. Between the extremes are many Italian balsamics with subtle flavors. As a rule, the more expensive the better, but try a few brands to find one you like.

BLOOD ORANGES Native to Sicily, blood oranges have a peel and flesh that can range in color from bright orange to deep red. Their juice is as sweet as that of navel and Valencia oranges, with a more intense flavor. Blood orange segments add spectacular color to salads and desserts. Once an exotic rarity, blood oranges are now becoming widely available during their winter harvest season.

BRAISING Meats and vegetables browned in a bit of oil, then simmered slowly with minimal liquid, develop superb flavor and texture. A braising pot should be heavy, to prevent scorching, with a tight lid, to retain moisture. Long, slow cooking tenderizes the connective tissue (collagen) in lean meats and the cellulose in fibrous vegetables.

BROWN RICE Because it retains its bran, brown rice is flavorful and a little chewy. Unlike white rice, it contains the grain's fiber, B vitamins, minerals, and oils. Brown Arborio is a creamy short-grain variety good in risotto. Brown Basmati is long-grain with a floral aroma. Wehani is also aromatic, with a nutty flavor. The bran's oils cause brown rice to spoil easily, so store airtight and use within months.

BUCKWHEAT GROATS Not a true grain, buckwheat, native to China, is the nutty-flavored seed of an annual herb related to sorrel and rhubarb. Whole seeds stripped of their inedible coating are called groats and are sold raw or toasted. Crushed groats, known as kasha, are served in side dishes and cereals. Buckwheat is also milled into flour and used in pancakes. Look for kasha and buckwheat flour in natural-foods stores.

BUTTERMILK Cow's milk to which a yogurt-like culture has been added, buttermilk is a tangy, slightly thick dairy product that is especially good as a mildly acidic ingredient in baked goods such as waffles and pancakes. Most buttermilk available now is made from low-fat or nonfat milk, but check to verify that the product has 2 percent or less butterfat. "Old-fashioned" versions are typically made with whole milk.

CAPERS These young, olive-green flower buds of the Mediterranean caper bush are unpleasantly bitter when raw, and so are always pickled in salty vinegar or packed in salt for eating. They have a peppery flavor that comes from mustard oils in the buds. Rinse and blot dry brined capers before use. Soak salt-packed ones for several minutes, then rinse and dry. Both preparations are excellent in pasta sauces and with fish and meats. Caper berries, similar in appearance to green olives, are immature fruits of the same plant, pickled and served as a condiment.

CHIFFONADE The culinary term for leafy fresh herbs or vegetables, such as basil, spinach, or lettuce, that have been cut into slender ribbons. To make a chiffonade, assemble the leaves to be cut into a neat stack, then fold or roll them lengthwise into a tight bundle. With a sharp kitchen knife, slice the stack crosswise into strips—thin for basil and other herbs, wider for large greens. Separate the ribbons before adding them to a dish. *See also* julienne.

CHILE PASTE A long-lived condiment easy to keep on hand, chile paste—made from hot red peppers mashed with salt and vinegar—can put a spicy Asian spin on basic dishes. It keeps indefinitely in the refrigerator.

CHILES Many markets now stock several kinds of fresh and dried chiles. Some, such as Anaheim, New Mexico, and poblano (called ancho when dried), are usually only mildly hot. Others, such as serranos and jalapeños, have been bred for hotness. Jalapeños smoked and then canned in a tomato sauce are sold as "chipotle chiles in adobo," and are used to give Mexican-style dishes a smoky hotness. They are best chopped finely or puréed. Freeze unused chipotles in an airtight container. With all chiles, the secret is to add them slowly and taste as you cook. For safety, wear rubber gloves or avoid touching your face until you've washed your hands and kitchen tools in hot, soapy water.

COOKING SPRAYS Simply oils of various kinds mixed with a small amount of alcohol and lecithin (an emulsifier) in a pressurized can, cooking sprays are convenient for applying a thin coating of oil to pans and utensils. Canola oil spray is nearly flavorless, while olive oil versions have a mild olive taste. Use them lightly and always spray away from open flames or burners.

CRYSTALLIZED GINGER Also known as candied ginger, crystallized ginger is sliced, peeled gingerroot that has been simmered in a sugar syrup and coated with coarse sugar. Sold in jars, it's handy for adding a note of sweet spiciness to both savory dishes and desserts.

DRIED CHERRIES Unlike raisins, which are simply grapes allowed to dry, dried cherries—typically made from a naturally tart variety—are sweetened with sugar, although they retain many of the fruit's nutrients.

DRIED COCONUT Sweetened varieties of dried coconut, available in supermarkets, are slightly moist and extremely sugary. Unsweetened versions, found in natural-foods stores and Asian markets, are drier and have a more pure coconut flavor. Both come shredded or flaked.

EGGS Although they've been treated as a virtual emblem of cholesterol-rich foods, eggs can fit into a healthy eating plan. Because the main causes of high blood cholesterol are animal fats and hydrogenated oils, some recommendations allow up to four eggs a week, unless your cholesterol is high, in which case it's advisable to eat just two a week.

ESCAROLE A member of the large family of edible greens that includes lettuce, radicchio, Belgian endive, and others, escarole grows in loose, pale heads of broad, somewhat frilly leaves. Its sweet but mildly bitter flavor is similar to endive's, and it can be served raw in a salad with other greens, or lightly cooked in soups or side dishes. Store in plastic in the refrigerator for up to 3 days.

FENNEL A fennel bulb is actually the white base of a tall, feathery-leaved plant in the carrot family. Its subtle licorice flavor makes it a pleasing addition to green salads, stews, and other dishes. Shop for crisp, white bulbs with bright green tops; strip away outer layers that are tough or browned.

FISH If you're a woman who is pregnant or nursing a baby or considering pregnancy, research suggests that you should eat no more than 12 ounces of fish a week, since many varieties contain small amounts of mercury. When the metal is consumed in a mother's meals, it can pose a risk to unborn children and breast-feeding infants. Pregnant women and very young children should not eat shark, swordfish, king mackerel, or tilefish, four kinds of fish that naturally contain unusually high amounts of this toxic metal.

FLAXSEED The tiny reddish brown seed of the flax plant, flaxseed—also known as linseed—is rich in omega-3 fatty acids, which appear to help lower heart disease risk. Flaxseed has a mild, nutty flavor that's good in baked goods and breakfast cereals. Because its oil spoils quickly, flaxseed should be stored airtight in the refrigerator or freezer and ground, if desired, just before use.

FOLDING EGG WHITES Beaten egg whites lose volume if simply stirred in common fashion into a batter. To keep the final dish light and airy, incorporate the whites by a method called folding. Using a rubber spatula, gently scrape stiff, just-beaten egg whites into the bowl holding the batter or other mixture. Gently plunge the spatula into the mixture and, with a scooping motion, fold the bottom of the batter up and over the top. Repeat, rotating the bowl after each fold, until just a few pale streaks remain. If the mixture is thick, stir in one-fourth of the egg whites to lighten it, then gently fold in the rest.

FRESH GINGER Found year-round in supermarkets, fresh ginger, or gingerroot, has a sweet, multilayered spiciness that surpasses the simple flavor of ground dried ginger. Its smooth skin must be peeled away, but peel gently—the flesh beneath is especially pungent, with a hotness unlike that of red or black pepper. Store unpeeled ginger in plastic in the refrigerator for up to 3 weeks or the freezer for up to a year.

FRESH HERBS Thyme and other fresh herbs, now widely sold by the bunch, may seem aromatic yet can be subtle. When cooking with them, always use the full quantity indicated in the recipe, and crush or chop the leaves to release their aromatic oils. Dried herbs, in contrast, often seem mild but may add aggressive flavors. When substituting dried for fresh herbs, use one-third of the amount.

JULIENNE The culinary term for vegetables cut evenly into matchstick-shaped strips. Raw or lightly cooked vegetables are first thinly sliced lengthwise (about the thickness of a coin), then stacked and again thinly sliced in neat parallel rows, producing slender strips that are square in cross section. These can be lined up and cut to any length desired. *See also* chiffonade.

LEAN MEATS To cut back on fat, look for "select" grade red meats, which are less fatty than those labeled "prime" or "choice." The leanest cuts have fewer than 5 grams of fat per 3½ ounces (100 g). For comparison, 3½ ounces of skinless chicken breast meat has 1.2 grams of fat; chicken thigh meat, 3.9 grams. The leanest beef cuts (select grade, trimmed of visible fat) include top round (2.5 g), tip round (3.2 g), eye of round (3.6 g), sirloin, (3.7 g), and top loin (4.5 g). For extra-lean ground beef, ask to have one of these cuts specially ground by a butcher. The leanest pork cuts include the tenderloin (3.4 g), top loin chop (5.3 g), and ham (5.4 g). The leanest lamb cut is the leg (4.5 g).

MUSHROOMS Beyond the common white and brown, or cremini, many varieties of mushroom are now under cultivation. Portobello mushrooms—hearty enough to stand in for beef—have exploded in popularity. Despite their Italianate name, portobellos are simply fully developed white or brown mushrooms, best used soon after purchase. Fresh enoki, oyster, shiitake, and straw mushrooms are also now widely available. Porcini, most often sold dried, have a strong, earthy flavor that adds depth and sophistication to pastas, gratins, risottos, and other dishes. (Milder fresh porcini are also available but are harder to find.) To rehydrate dried porcini, place the mushroom pieces in a bowl and add boiling water to cover. Let stand for 5 minutes, then pour the soaking liquid through a fine-mesh sieve into another bowl. In a colander, rinse the softened mushrooms. Use both the mushrooms and liquid to taste. While treasured mainly for their woodsy flavors, mushrooms are also an excellent source of niacin and a good source of riboflavin.

NAPA CABBAGE Also known as Chinese cabbage, napa cabbage has white ribs and pale yellow to pale green crinkly leaves formed in loose, oblong heads about the size of romaine (cos) lettuce heads. It is crisp and sweet, with a flavor that is milder than that of green and red cabbages. Use shredded napa cabbage in salads, soups, or side dishes.

NUTMEG Because the singular aroma and flavor of this spice come from volatile compounds that dissipate quickly, nutmeg that is freshly grated adds more to a dish than does the ground nutmeg sold in jars. Whole nutmeg is readily available in supermarket spice racks, and small, inexpensive graters designed specifically for nutmeg help produce the fine grains that look and taste best.

OLIVE OIL Of the many vegetable oils used for cooking, olive oil has the widest range of flavors—bland, buttery, sweet, peppery, grassy. Keep at least two types on hand: a mild, low-cost variety for sautéing and roasting, and a quality extra-virgin for salads and other dishes in which the oil is central. An extra-virgin's flavor is not evident in its color or price, so taste a few to find one you like. Olive oils are rich in healthful monounsaturated fats.

OLIVES Where supermarkets once offered only jumbo black and pimiento-stuffed green olives, they now shelve a widening array of domestic and imported olives. Commonly available are brine-cured Niçoise, Kalamata, and Greek black olives, as well as heavily seasoned Sicilian and other Italian-style green olives. Find more exotic varieties, such as French picholines and Spanish arbequinas, at specialty-food stores.

PARMESAN CHEESE Supermarkets now typically carry a variety of foreign and domestic Parmesan cheeses, but the version widely considered to have the most complex and appealing flavor is Parmigiano-Reggiano, an aged cow's-milk cheese named for the Italian provinces of Parma and Reggio Emilia. Although all Parmesans are quite salty, a small amount can add great depth of flavor to a dish, especially when the cheese is top quality, purchased in block form, and grated by hand just before serving.

PARSLEY Mild curly-leaf parsley is the traditional favorite, but flavorful flat-leaf, or Italian, parsley is gaining in popularity. Renowned as a decorative garnish, parsley also deserves respect as a nutritious vegetable. One-fourth of a cup of chopped parsley has as much vitamin C as a whole cup of romaine lettuce. Parsley also contains calcium, potassium, and folate.

PEARL ONIONS About the size of a grape or an olive, tiny white pearl onions are mild and sweet when cooked. Boiling onions, also mild and white-skinned, are a bit larger, typically around 1 inch (2.5 cm) across. To peel pearl or boiling onions, bring a saucepan half full of water to a boil, add the onions, and cook for 1–2 minutes, depending on their size. With a slotted spoon, transfer the onions to a large bowl partially filled with ice water. When the onions are cool, remove and squeeze each at its root end; the skin should slide off in one piece.

PEELING TOMATOES Fill a pan with enough water to cover the tomatoes and bring to a boil. Using a small, sharp knife, cut out the core from each tomato's stem end. Cut a shallow X in the other end. Submerge in the boiling water until the skin wrinkles, about 20 seconds. Using a slotted spoon, transfer to a bowl of cold water. Peel when cool. Cut in half crosswise, then squeeze gently and shake to dislodge the seeds.

PINE NUTS Excellent raw or toasted, these small, ivory-colored nuts are the shelled seeds of several varieties of pine tree, treasured for their subtle flavor. Ground finely and blended with basil, olive oil, and garlic, they are a crucial ingredient in tradi-tional Italian pesto. They are also delicious toasted and sprinkled whole or chopped on salads and side dishes, or baked into tarts and cookies.

PLUM TOMATOES With their dense flesh and scant juice, egg-shaped plum tomatoes, also known as Italian or Roma tomatoes, are ideal for pasta sauces and cooked dishes. For smooth sauces, peel and seed plum tomatoes before use (see left); for best flavor, store all varieties at room temperature.

POTATOES Waxy round red and white potatoes (called new potatoes or creamers when small) are moist and firm and are the best choice for salads and soups. Starchy russet, long white, and purple- and yellow-fleshed potatoes turn crumbly during cooking and are best mashed or baked. Potatoes contain potassium, vitamin C, and iron.

QUESO ASADERO A commonly available Mexican-style melting cheese, *queso asadero* is slightly lower in fat than similar cheeses, such as Monterey jack.

RACK OF LAMB, FRENCHED The cut of lamb called a rack typically yields six to eight tiny but flavorful rib chops. For ease of serving and elegance of presentation after roasting, the rack should be frenched beforehand. This preparation, done by the butcher, involves trimming any meat and fat from between the ribs, leaving the rib-eye meat intact, then scraping the rib bones clean. Once roasted, the rack is cut into individual bone-in chops and served.

ROASTING BELL PEPPERS Preheat the broiler (grill). Position the rack 4 inches (10 cm) from the heat source. Place the pepper (capsicum) on a baking sheet lined with aluminum foil. Broil (grill), turning frequently with tongs, until the skin blackens all over, about 10 minutes. Transfer the pepper to a bowl, cover, and let steam until the skin loosens, about 10 minutes. Peel, cover, and refrigerate until needed.

SAFFRON With its stunning golden hue and distinctive, earthy taste, saffron earns its place in the kitchen. Each slender saffron thread is plucked by hand from the center of a small crocus flower, making it one of the world's priciest spices. Only a tiny amount is needed, however, to give a dish evident color and character. For the best flavor, purchase saffron as threads, not powder, and steep them in hot water for several minutes before using.

SESAME OIL Plain sesame oil, pressed from untoasted seeds, is mild and nearly colorless. It is an excellent cooking oil, widely used in Asia and the Middle East. More widely available is roasted, or Asian, sesame oil. Made from toasted sesame seeds, it is pale to medium brown with a strong flavor and is best used with a light hand as a seasoning, not as a salad or cooking oil. Store roasted sesame oil in the refrigerator; use within 6 months.

SESAME SEEDS Raw sesame seeds are mild and faintly sweet, but when toasted they turn a golden color with a rich, nutty, and slightly bitter flavor. Black sesame seeds, with their dark hulls, or outer coverings, are widely used as a garnish in Japanese and Chinese cooking. (The seeds inside are a pale ivory color, with the usual crunch and mild flavor.) To toast sesame seeds, heat a small frying pan over medium-high heat, then add the seeds and toast, stirring, until the seeds are light brown and starting to crackle, 3–5 minutes. Always toast seeds just before using. Sesame seeds are rich in polyunsaturated oil, which can spoil over time; store untoasted seeds in an airtight container in the refrigerator for up to 6 months.

SHALLOTS Their tan, papery skins and pungent, layered flesh show that shallots are related to onions. They grow in loose clusters of small cloves, however, and have a distinctive flavor that some describe as midway between onion and garlic. Shallots are often used chopped or minced as a seasoning in sauces and vinaigrettes, but can be sliced and sautéed like yellow onions.

SHRIMP For years, seafood lovers were counseled to reduce their cholesterol intake by cutting back on shrimp (or prawns, as some sizes and varieties are known). Although shellfish vary, shrimp on average have twice as much cholesterol as dark-meat chicken. However, the chief cause of clogged arteries is the saturated fat in food, not the cholesterol. Eight large shrimp contain just 85 milligrams of cholesterol and less than 1 gram of fat, only a fraction of which is saturated. In other words, there's no good reason for shrimp to be banned from the kitchens of health-minded cooks.

SOY MILK Made from soybeans that have been cooked, mashed, and strained, soy milk has a flavor and texture much like ordinary milk but with a nutrition profile like that of the bean itself: respectable amounts of protein and unsaturated fat, along with compounds that appear to fight cardiovascular disease and cancer. It can be used cup for cup in place of milk in most recipes.

SUMMER SQUASH Prized for their mild flesh, thin skin, and edible seeds, summer squash are most tender and sweet when small. Crookneck, pattypan, and zucchini (courgettes) are popular examples, but more exotic varieties such as chayote (mirliton), ronde de Nice, and others have begun to appear in markets. Refrigerate in plastic for up to 5 days.

SUN-DRIED TOMATOES Once an exotic Italian specialty, sun-dried tomatoes are now sold widely in a variety of forms. To avoid the extra helping of fat in oil-packed versions, shop for dry-packed tomatoes, available leather-dry in plastic bags or tubs, or slightly moist in antiseptic vacuum packs. To reconstitute sun-dried tomatoes before use, place them in a bowl and add boiling water to cover. Let stand until softened, about 5 minutes, then drain.

TOASTING NUTS To add flavor and crunch to nuts, place a small amount in a small, dry frying pan over medium-low heat and toast, stirring constantly, until golden brown and fragrant, 3–5 minutes. Or spread larger quantities on a baking sheet and toast in a 350°F (180°C) oven, stirring often, until lightly browned, 8–10 minutes. Transfer to a plate to cool. The same method can be used to toast raw sesame seeds.

TOFU Made of cooked soybeans, tofu comes in a range of textures, making the bean curd an adaptable ingredient. Firm and extra-firm tofu, like chicken, picks up flavors in stir-fries and on the grill. Soft tofu is ideal for blending with other ingredients in soups and smoothies. Creamy silken tofu is perfect for custardy desserts. All tofu is rich in protein and a source of B vitamins and iron.

TURBINADO SUGAR Pale brown or blond with coarse, dry crystals, turbinado sugar is a partially purified form of raw sugar, manufactured from the residue left when sugar cane is processed into granulated white sugar and molasses. Preferred for some recipes for its mild molasses flavor, it can be used interchangeably with granulated sugar in most dishes.

VANILLA Many cooks keep two kinds of vanilla on hand: whole vanilla beans, the aromatic, coffee-colored seed pods of a tropical orchid, and pure vanilla extract (essence), a dark liquid made by steeping the beans in alcohol. The beans, mainly from Madagascar, are expensive but more flavorful than the extract. To use vanilla beans, slit them lengthwise with a small, sharp knife and scrape out the tiny dark seeds. Add the seeds to desserts, cookie and pastry doughs, and sauces.

WALNUT OIL Pressed from walnuts that have been lightly toasted, walnut oil has a pleasing flavor like that of the nuts themselves. It is best used as a flavor enhancer, not a principal ingredient, in salads and side dishes, especially those containing toasted walnuts. Because walnut oil spoils readily, it should be purchased in small quantities and stored in the refrigerator.

WHEAT GERM Renowned as a healthy food, wheat germ is the grain's unsprouted green bud, or embryo, which is lost, along with the fiber-rich bran, during processing. It contains a big portion of the wheat seed's proteins, minerals, and vitamins, including vitamin E. Raw or toasted (both kinds are available), the germ has a crunchy texture and nutty flavor that's delicious in breads and cereals. Because of its oil, which can spoil, wheat germ should be bought in small quantities and stored in an airtight container in the refrigerator.

WHOLE-WHEAT FLOUR Milled from wheat kernels that contain their original bran and germ, or embryo, whole-wheat (wholemeal) flour is nutritionally superior to white flour, with more fiber, more vitamins and minerals, and a bit of heart-healthy oil. It's also more flavorful. But since its trace of oil can spoil, it should be bought in small quantities and stored in a sealed container in the refrigerator. It will keep for up to 6 months.

Vegetable Stock

Fat-free, reduced-sodium canned broth is an acceptable substitute for this delicious homemade stock.

3 teaspoons olive oil

12–14 fresh white mushrooms, coarsely chopped

1 large yellow onion, cut into 1-inch (2.5-cm) pieces

3 large carrots, cut into 1-inch (2.5-cm) pieces

2 celery stalks with leaves, cut into 1-inch (2.5-cm) pieces

6 cloves garlic, halved

8 cups (64 fl oz/2 l) water

6 fresh flat-leaf (Italian) parsley sprigs

4 fresh thyme sprigs

1 bay leaf

⅛ teaspoon salt

In a stockpot, heat 2 teaspoons of the olive oil over medium-high heat. Add the mushrooms and sauté until they begin to brown, 4–5 minutes. Push the mushrooms to the side and add the remaining 1 teaspoon oil, the onion, carrots, celery, and garlic. Raise the heat to high and sauté, stirring often, until the vegetables are deeply browned, about 10 minutes. Add the water, parsley, thyme, bay leaf, and salt. Bring to a boil, then reduce the heat to medium-low and simmer, uncovered, for 25–30 minutes. Remove from the heat and let cool slightly. Strain the stock into a bowl through a sieve lined with paper towels. Use immediately, cover and refrigerate for up to 3 days, or freeze airtight for up to 3 months.

MAKES ABOUT 6 CUPS (48 fl oz/1.5 l)

INDEX

MAYO CLINIC

Co-editors: Donald Hensrud, M.D.; Jennifer Nelson, R.D.
Editor in Chief, Books and Newsletters: Christopher Frye
Contributing Editor: Nicole Spelhaug
Product Marketing Manager: Rebecca Roberts

WELDON OWEN INC.

Chief Executive Officer: John Owen
President: Terry Newell
Chief Operating Officer: Larry Partington
Vice President International Sales: Stuart Laurence
Creative Director: Gaye Allen
Associate Creative Director: Leslie Harrington
Associate Publisher: Val Cipollone
Managing Editor: Sheridan Warrick
Designer and Photography Director: Julia Flagg
Assistant Editor: Mitch Goldman
Contributing Writer: Peter Jaret
Copy Editors: Carrie Bradley, Sharon Silva
Production Director: Chris Hemesath
Color Specialist: Teri Bell
Production Coordinator: Libby Temple
Proofreaders: Desne Ahlers, Arin Hailey
Indexer: Ken DellaPenta
Food Stylist: Dan Becker
Prop Stylist: Leigh Noë

ACKNOWLEDGMENTS

Special thanks to Kyrie Forbes, Joan Olson,
Guarina Lopez, Jessica Giblin, and
Catherine Jacobes for their creative contribution
and valuable assistance.

THE NEW MAYO CLINIC COOKBOOK
CONCISE EDITION

Conceived and produced by
WELDON OWEN INC.
814 Montgomery Street, San Francisco, CA 94133
Telephone: 415-291-0100 Fax: 415-291-8841
and
MAYO CLINIC HEALTH INFORMATION
200 First Street, SW
Rochester, MN 55905

TRADEMARKS

MAYO, MAYO CLINIC, MAYO CLINIC HEALTH INFORMATION,
the triple-shield Mayo logo, and MAYO CLINIC HEALTHY WEIGHT
PYRAMID are marks of Mayo Foundation for
Medical Education and Research.

For reliable health information, go to www.MayoClinic.com,
Mayo Clinic Health Information's Web site.

A WELDON OWEN PRODUCTION

First printed in 2004
10 9 8 7 6 5 4 3 2 1

ISBN: 1-893005-36-4

Printed by Midas Printing Limited
Printed in China

A NOTE ON WEIGHTS AND MEASURES

All recipes include customary U.S. and metric measurements. Metric conversions are based
on a standard developed for this book and have been rounded off. Actual weights may vary.